# NO RELATION

## Christina Reis

Front and back covers design copyright

© 2021

Kevin Farrell

First edition published by Silver Quill Publishing 2021

***www.christinareis***.co.uk

ISBN: 978-1-912513-38-3

UK spelling observed

Typeset in Georgia

Silver Quill Publishing

*https://www.silverquillpublishing.com*

Denise Read.

**Dedicated to...**

**My children, who always believed in me.**

*Once upon a time there were two girls, who met briefly, for one time only, but whose lives became inextricably entwined. This is their story*

# CHAPTER 1

## *March 1976*

It was a lovely night, fresh, clear, sharp and brightened by a moon just a shaving less than full. Laurel stood for a moment, looking around, imprinting the experience on her mind. She was so happy she could burst. Then she turned and knocked softly on the window, breaking the spell.

"Fid!" she whispered. "Fid, let me in!" The shabby old house usually looked bare and dowdy, as if no one actually lived there, but tonight, the house and the whole world was warm and welcoming. So was Fid as she scurried to the window, struggling into a thin nylon negligee that matched her yellow nightie, her long red hair untidy and matted at the back.

"Well? Laurel, tell me!" Fidelma's large green eyes stared expectantly into her friend's animated face as she opened the window.

Laurel's long, dark brown legs cleared the sill easily and she slid noiselessly into the room. "He loves me, Fid. He said he's in love with me! Oh God, it's so exciting!" Laurel grabbed Fid's hands and whirled her round in a crazy little dance.

"Shush, be quiet! You'll wake the nuns. Sure, you can tell me all in the morning." Her soft Irish tones were soothing and indulgent.

"Ok. That's if we get the chance."

"We'll make the chance, I promise."

Fid went back to bed, leaving Laurel to relive her magical night. She was almost sixteen and soon she would be allowed to leave the children's home she had lived in since she started school. Life had taken on a new meaning since Fid had come to work at the home. She had never had such a close friend before. Social workers would visit from time to time to ask after her welfare, and the nuns ran the house, but she couldn't talk to them like she confided in Fid. Fid's life had been so different to Laurel's. Laurel had no family, whereas Fid was brought up in Ireland with her brothers and sisters. Her live-in cleaning job at the home was only allowed by her parents because it involved the Church.

Fid had a boyfriend whom she knew as a child and who came to England on the same boat. They were both eighteen and he lived with his parents. They were allowed to 'walk out' together once a week.

In contrast to Fid's life being surrounded by family, Laurel could just about remember her mother, her only known relative. Somewhere, amongst the bottom pile of her memories she could still see the dark-brown arm alongside her own, smell her scented-soap skin and feel the soft, springy cushion of her hair. It was a happy memory, full of feelings of safety and love. The older children at the home frequently told her that her mother used to come and see her and that she screamed and punched and kicked her mother when she tried to leave. But she could not remember any of that.

Every now and then, the nuns or the carers at the home would bring her a parcel containing a toy, saying it had been sent to her through the post, by her mother. But the other children had noticed a strange black woman in old clothes and fuzzy hair, peering over the gate. They saw her throw a parcel over the wall. Laurel was certain this strange person was not her mother. But the others jeered and taunted her until she gave the toy away. Now that she was almost sixteen, these older children had long since left to make their own way in the world.

Laurel would soon be following them. Try as she might, she couldn't recall the last time a present came for her. The nuns and the carers had changed so many times there was no one left to tell her. She had always felt an outsider in the world until Fid came to work at the house. It was great to have a friend she could see every day. Her school friends' lives were so different than hers that it was difficult to feel part of their crowd. In the small industrial town there were few black faces, and everyone she knew outside the children's home had a family. They all knew where they came from, so she not only looked different, she felt different. Now she had a boyfriend she was one of the gang.

A few days later, Laurel rushed excitedly into the toilet block as Fid was cleaning. Laurel's tall, gangly body filled the doorway, dwarfing Fid's slight frame. "Guess what? Carl wants to come out with us." Laurel's big eyes brimmed with pleasure. "When's your day off? He wants to go to McDonald's. It's a new café just opened. He knows all about it. There's lots of them in other places. We're the last ones to get one. You could bring Sean."

Fid was curious about Carl. They had been at the cinema together, Fid, Sean and Laurel, when the couple met. Carl had left the gang of boys he was with and come over to sit with them. He addressed most of his conversation to Laurel on that occasion. Both the girls' ideas about romance were gleaned from magazines and films, and this chance meeting was to them, the start of a great love affair. Fid believed that she would be with Sean forever, so this was as near as she would get to real-life passion.

The following Saturday they showed up at McDonald's. Carl was already there, dressed in the latest fashion, blonde hair long and well brushed and reeking of aftershave. He was small and slim with a self-confident attitude only an eighteen-year-old could pull off. His platform shoes brought him up to somewhere near Laurel's height. He made no attempt to hide the fact that he felt superior to these country bumpkins from Ireland. "And what do you do, Sean? I know Fid's the cleaner." He cast a condescending look their way, his arm possessively around Laurel's shoulder.

"I'm a gardener. I work with my father," Sean mumbled shyly, his head down and massive arms and hands folded on the table.

3

"A gardener! Well, I'm in business. Buying and selling and all that." He beamed a self-satisfied smile round the room.

"He's got a lot of things going. He's very clever." Laurel gazed admiringly at him. "He's got plans. Someday he'll be rich."

"I'm well off now. Enough to buy us all lunch." He pulled a ten-pound note from his pocket.

"Well? Care to order?" He sauntered to the counter. "Can you change this?" he asked casually to the assistant.

"What do you think?" asked Laurel. He was only a few feet away, but the noise in the crowded restaurant put him out of earshot.

"Er... he seems to know lots of things," Fid volunteered.

"It's good of him to pay for the burgers," said Sean carefully.

Laurel laughed happily. "You'll like him when you get used to him. He likes showing off, but he's very kind, really."

They all strolled back to the home together. Laurel's room was next door to Fid's. Both were tiny, but Laurel loved that room. As she was the eldest girl, she had the privilege of a room to herself. The other girls slept in a dormitory and it was sheer luck that there was no room for her in there, so a little bolthole of her own was a very special commodity. Fid's room was a precious sanctuary for her too, as at home in Ireland she had ten brothers and sisters. A live-in job was wonderful and she didn't intend to be a cleaner all her life. She had plans as well, but certainly didn't want to share them with Carl. She hoped to be a hairdresser and was saving to go to college.

They reached the gate. Sean and Fid kissed a chaste goodbye. They all watched his large, strong frame disappearing down the road. Carl hung around and eventually said to Laurel, "Sneak out after tea and we'll go for a walk. I'll be waiting on the corner." He did not wait for an answer and set off with a jaunty swagger. After a few yards he waved without turning round, confident the girls were still watching him.

At bedtime, Fid crept into Laurel's room. It was empty and the sash window had been opened to a mere fingertip's breadth. Fid lay awake in her own room for a few minutes, listening for her friend's return. However she fell asleep hours before a flushed and dishevelled Laurel prised open the window and curled up in bed to dream about her wonderful lover.

Saturday nights became a regular routine for Laurel. Afternoons were spent at the cinema and at McDonald's and evenings at the window watching for Carl's arrival. He would walk past the gate to signal he was there and Laurel would climb out of the window to join him round the corner.

Twenty-five years ago, a religious order had started the children's home, which in those days was called an orphanage, and the nuns ran a harsh regime. Now they still lived there and managed the domestic affairs, but there were a few secular employees to care for the children and a social worker to supervise the children's welfare. Many rules had been relaxed over the years, but one remained with no hope of repeal. Every Sunday morning residents and staff attended the church service next door. Dragging herself from a warm bed after very little sleep was the worst part of the weekend. Father Michael was middle-aged and well meaning, but his sermons were rambling and full of big words. Kneeling down for prayers was a bit of a hazard as well. There was a real danger of falling asleep in that position and remaining there when everyone else stood up. But it was a small price to pay. Saturday nights were worth it.

One Saturday afternoon, as the four of them walked back from the town centre, Carl told them to get away early the following Saturday.

"Why, what's going on?" asked Laurel eagerly.

"I've got a bit of money coming. I thought I might take us all to Belle Vue."

5

The three of them stared back at him, then at each other. At last, Fid said, "Sure, and where's that in the big wide world?"

"Never heard of Belle Vue?" Carl's superiority was assured. "It's two buses away, that's all. It's time you lot saw the sights. There's more to life than the pictures."

"Well, what is it?" Laurel persisted.

"It's everything you could want for a day out, that's what. You'll love it!"

The three innocents gathered round him in awe as he described the attractions of the amusement park.

"It must cost a pretty penny," Sean, ever practical, added suspiciously.

"I've told you I've got a bit of money coming. I'll pay." Carl was enjoying the attention and the power. His friends' eyes lit up in excitement.

Laurel could hardly concentrate in school and spent every spare minute fantasising about it. Fid sought her out to chat about it every chance she got, and even Sean, usually reticent and shy, couldn't help telling his parents how much he was looking forward to it.

They were not disappointed. They were lucky enough to have a beautiful day. The zoo park was bathed in sunlight, so all the animals came out to be admired. How big and dangerous they looked. Even mild, good-natured creatures like giraffes and elephants seemed threatening in real life to people who had only seen them in story books. Watching lions and tigers gave them a thrill they'd never experienced before.

All the pent-up fear was released by screaming their way down the water flume and the scenic railway in the amusement park. Then they paddled their way round the boating lake in pairs, shrieking when they bumped into each other. Carl tried to stay aloof and sophisticated, but he could not help showing he was having fun. True to his word, he paid for everything, including fish and chips at tea time. No one dared question where the money came from, though they all wondered.

They were sitting on the grass, eating and chatting, when a man taking photographs approached. "Want a picture? Nice photo of the four of you? Only 90 pence."

He pointed his camera without waiting for a reply. Carl was about to refuse, but Sean cut in. "Yes, why not? I'll pay. You've paid for everything. It's very kind of you, so it is."

The photographer seized his moment. "Say cheese! Here, fill this in with your name and address." It was done before they realised anything was happening. He was already eyeing up another family of potential customers as Sean filled in the form. He snatched the money and the details and was gone, his retreating back view scurrying towards his next customer.

They were dressed in their best clothes. Fid and Laurel were in pretty mini-dresses and Carl as usual was wearing flared trousers, boots and a fitted shirt. Only Sean let them down in a suit that used to be his father's. There was a dance hall in the park, but Laurel could not stay out that late without getting into trouble, much as she wanted to. As they strolled to the bus stop, a Rolling Stones number came through the loudspeaker. Laurel held onto Fid's arms and danced up the road, oblivious to glances of amusement or disapproval. They reached the bus stop, shrieking with laughter. Sean and Carl exchanged a look of embarrassment. It was the first and last time they shared an emotion. The girls didn't even notice their disapproval.

A few days later, Sean gave Laurel the photo. It was a memento of the happiest day of her life.

Apart from that magical weekend, Saturdays became a regular routine for Laurel: afternoons at the cinema and evenings at the window watching for Carl's signal to slip out of the window and join him. Nothing quite lived up to that glorious day, but it was a happy time, nonetheless.

One Saturday night he told her he would not be there the next week. "I'm off to London. I've met some friends and they're giving me a job down there."

"That's exciting!" London seemed a far-off, exotic place compared to their small northern town.

"When will you be back?"

"Dunno. Won't be gone long. May be a couple of weeks."

"I'd love to go to London!" It felt as if her world was opening up. "Take me with you! I'm nearly sixteen. When I'm sixteen I can go where I like!"

"I'll come back soon. If it goes ok, maybe we can go down there to live. Watch for me. I'll pass the gate, like always."

"When?"

"In a few Saturdays. As long as it takes."

They were on the corner. "Got to go, now." He kissed her goodbye and she clung to him, trying not to waste a second of his presence. He pulled himself away with a smile and set off down the road, with a backward wave, as usual. Laurel watched until he was out of sight. The thought of a new life in London was thrilling, but how could she carry on without her precious Saturday nights?

Fid was comforting. "Two Saturdays aren't that bad. You can always come out with Sean and me."

But two, then three, then four Saturdays came and went without a sign of Carl. Every Saturday night she sat in the window and watched for him. She realised that she had no idea where he lived or worked. He was adept at concealing details about himself. Laurel had never even asked his last name. But then, he didn't know hers. To ease the pain she would think about their meetings and how good they were. Sunday mornings in church became a time to dream of happy times while the long sermon was in progress. It was a hot summer and the cool air inside was a relief. The children suffered in winter as the temperature in the high-roofed stone building never really altered with the seasons. It was usually only a quarter full with worshippers, so human heat did not warm it up. But summer services were pleasant. It was a time to relax in a cool, peaceful building.

The end of term was approaching and a hostel was being sought for Laurel to move into after her birthday in August. She was looking forward to having Carl round instead of sneaking out in secret. If he came back after she left, at least Fid would know where she was. But he would be back long before then, wouldn't he?

# CHAPTER 2

## *May 1976*

It was Karen's wedding day. It wasn't a bit like the day of her childhood dreams, or like her friends' big days. There were no church bells or choir or flower girls or even bridesmaids. The little registry office was clean and tidy, but hardly festive. There was no father to give her away because they had lost touch years ago. They had never been close, especially after her mother died. Ben's father was sweet and kindly and loved Karen dearly, but he was too elderly and frail to make the short journey from London to the northwest, and Ben's mum had to stay to look after him. The newly-weds planned to spend their honeymoon staying with his parents in their Clapham council flat.

The whole affair may have seemed strange to the well-to-do colleagues of her father, but Karen had never felt happier than she did as she walked to the registry office hand-in-hand with Ben. Their friends from the art school where they both worked followed them. Most of them had stayed the night at the couple's new flat to help them move in. Every penny they had went into the purchase of the top floor of a big old house in a leafy avenue outside the town centre. They both preferred to spend money on the home rather than the wedding.

Despite the small budget, Karen looked radiant that day. Long golden curls fell to her shoulders and she wore an ankle-length cream dress made of cheesecloth, plain except for a huge single sunflower embroidered from neckline to hem. Someone brought a bunch of yellow roses from the garden and wrapped them in paper decorated with horseshoes. She put one in her hair and carried the rest, and her outfit was complete.

The ceremony was short but poignant. Karen felt she was melting when she looked into Ben's eyes, calm and kindly like his father's. They had no words for each other but shared their thoughts by their expressions.

Karen was so small and slight that everyone had to stoop to kiss the bride, and Ben was so tall that everyone had to stand on tiptoe to kiss the groom. Afterwards the wedding party went off to the pub, where one of their friends had brought sandwiches, sausage rolls and pies. The juke box was playing a Hot Chocolate number and everyone began singing "I believe in miracles. Where you from, you sexy thing!" and screaming with laughter. They stayed until the towels went on the pumps and then trooped back to the flat to play music on the stereo record player that their friends had clubbed together to give them as their wedding present. When the last person had staggered home, Ben and Karen fell into bed, elated and exhausted.

"What do you think? Was it alright?" Ben asked tentatively of his new bride.

"It was perfect, Ben. I couldn't have asked for more love and support."

"I can't help it if your parents aren't here for you, but I'll do my best to make up for that. I'll look after you." As he said the words, he realised that his resourceful and capable little bride would be hell-bent on looking after him.

He knew that she thought he was too nice and was often taken advantage of. But she replied softly, "I know you will. I've never doubted it. You know how I hated Dad's wedding with all those people I didn't know and everyone being politely catty to everyone else. I didn't know it could be such a loving, joyous occasion. That is, until now."

"Did you tell anyone you were pregnant?" Ben asked.

"No, not yet. It's still our secret. I can hardly believe it myself."

"I'm the same. It's more than I dared hope for." He kissed the top of Karen's head which was nestled in his chest.

11

Love and pride filled Ben's mind and silenced him for a few moments. Then he tried to articulate his happiness, but she'd fallen asleep in his arms.

"Goodnight, Mrs Moss," he whispered softly. "I'm here now. You're safe."

# CHAPTER 3

Sex was never talked about by Laurel's elders. The biology lessons in school referred briefly to the human genital organs and a well-meaning carer prepared her before her periods started, but intercourse was never mentioned. Going with boys was not allowed but never elaborated on. However, it was a subject that was freely discussed amongst the children, some of whom came from families where such matters were common knowledge.

"Don't you want that pickle?" Mary, a nosey twelve-year-old, shoved Laurel's favourite relish under her nose during tea. Laurel cringed and turned away. "You don't do you? You don't like it anymore." She plonked a spoonful of the stuff on Laurel's plate and watched the reaction with great interest. The smell made Laurel so nauseous she had to run out to the toilet. When she returned, Mary had a triumphant look on her face. "You're up the duff, aren't you?"

Laurel did not answer.

"When's your curse due?"

Still no answer.

"You've been shagging somebody. I can tell. I could tell when my sister got pregnant. I used to do that pickle thing to her."

"Why?"

"To get her back, of course. She was dead bossy to me. Anyway, you need to sort it out. Otherwise it might be too late to get rid."

Laurel was baffled. "Why would I do that?"

"I dunno. So you won't get saddled with a bawling kid. Well, that's what my mum said to my sister. It was my mum's boyfriend that did it."

Laurel looked blankly at Mary, reluctant to say any more in case it prompted further questions.

"It's a mortal sin, you know, shagging. The nuns will send you straight to hell." She smirked across at Laurel and moved the pickle nearer. "Mum's boyfriend tried it on with me, but I pushed him off. Mum was told to throw him out, but she wouldn't. That's why I'm in here."

She watched Laurel's face change and gave a satisfied smile. "Told you. You're well up the duff. You wait till the social worker finds out. She'll take it off you, even if you have it. But she'll try and make you get rid, without the nuns getting wind of it. I know. It happened to someone at my last place."

Laurel turned away without comment. This was news indeed. If Mary was right, she might have her own little baby! It was better to say nothing if she could be forced to give it up, or worse. Mary would be moving on soon, to a foster family. As long as she denied it, she was safe.

That night, alone in her room, she took out the picture and stared at it, trying to imagine what a baby of theirs would look like. Carl had turned his head away at the last moment but there was just enough of his profile to show his features. His blonde hair curved round his cheek and neck and fell into a fringe on his forehead. An aching feeling caught her unawares and suddenly she felt an intense longing to see him. Perhaps this Saturday he would be back.

But the weeks passed with no sign of him and the sickly feeling went. Mary left the home to go to a foster family and Laurel felt much better. It had been a stomach bug or something. She never had regular periods anyway, so their absence meant nothing. She said nothing to Fid, and life at school and home went on as usual.

A few days before she left school, a job became vacant at the local Woolworth's. Now she would have her own money! Her teachers advised her to come back to school in the autumn to study 'A' levels, and there was a place for her at a nearby hostel as soon as the present occupant moved out. Life was getting easier and more exciting. On her sixteenth birthday, she started work as a shop assistant. The other employees were a happy bunch and the supervisors much more relaxed than the harsh regime at the home and at school. Laurel was content especially when a wage packet arrived. Going back to do 'A' levels seemed less and less attractive. Fid and Sean took her out with them every Saturday and her teenage heart began to mend. However, the first thing she bought with her wages was a frame for the Belle Vue photograph, ready for the table in the new room she was looking forward to.

Then one day she was sitting in Fid's room, chatting about a night in the cinema the previous week when a strange sensation in her stomach made her rub it, almost subconsciously.

"Why did you do that?" Fid asked curiously.

"What?"

"Touch your belly."

"I didn't know I did. It just feels a bit strange, that's all. Kind of windy."

Laurel was wearing her shop overall which was loose and shapeless. Fid leaned over and ran a hand across Laurel's stomach. "Holy Mother of God!"

"What?"

"Don't you know what? You're pregnant!"

"No, I'm not. I thought I might be because I felt a bit sick a few weeks ago, but then it went away."

"Sure, there's a baby in there! I should know, I've got ten brothers and sisters. It's pregnant you are, and no mistake. You never told me that's what you and Carl were doing!"

"I didn't think to mention it. You never tell me what you and Sean are doing, so I thought you wouldn't want to talk about it!"

"We don't do it, that's why. Where we come from there's eyes watching you all the time. If you're a bad girl, everyone knows and you have to leave the village. A boy's not even supposed to see your tits!"

"Carl said it's what everyone does."

"Only if you're married!" Fid's green eyes widened in horror and concern. "You'll be an unmarried mother. Carl may not come back in time to marry you."

15

But Laurel, far from being terrified for the future, was smiling. "I can hardly believe it," she said in wonder. "I'm going to have a little baby of my own. I'll belong to somebody, and it'll belong to me."

"They'll make you give it away. That's what they do."

"I won't tell them. I won't tell anyone. Nobody knows except you."

"They soon will!" Fid retorted. "You're lucky you're in that uniform all day."

"I don't want them to take it away. I'll look after it. I've got a job. I'll have a place in the hostel soon. Fid, I so want this, more than I want Carl, even."

Fid looked at her friend. Her face was eager and hopeful. She had never seen her so alive since the day that Carl told her he loved her. Despite misgivings, she was happy for her. Perhaps, between them, they could make it work.

"We'll have to hide the bump. Perhaps you could move away. I'll help you look after it. We can take it in turns to work. I'll get a job at your place."

"Oh Fid, you are so good to me! I'm so lucky to have you!" Laurel jumped up to hug her friend. They both felt a movement on Laurel's stomach. "What's that?" Laurel asked in alarm.

"It's a kick, you eejit! That's what babies do when they're inside. I've felt my brothers and sisters kicking lots of times. It's going to get much bigger and so will you. We'll buy you some kind of corset to wear under your uniform."

"What will I do when it comes out?"

"We can tell them that we've got a plan to manage everything, so they can't make you give it away."

Innocently, they discussed the childcare together with no worries about sleepless nights, financial problems or childhood illnesses. The discomfort of labour and birth did not enter Laurel's head that day.

After a while, Fid asked tentatively, "What was it like, the sex? You know, the act? Sometimes I really want to do

16

it with Sean, but we'd both feel so guilty. We even feel guilty wanting to do it."

"Well, at first it was a bit of a let-down. I thought I really wanted it, but when I got it, it wasn't that great. It's not like it says in books or on the films. I only carried on because Carl seemed to enjoy it so much. But after a while, it got better and better and I felt really good afterwards. I looked forward to it, but as soon as I got to love it, Carl went off to London and it was hard to go back to normal again."

"Perhaps he'll be back in time to marry you. You're sixteen now, you can get married. In Ireland, he'd have to do it."

"Even if he doesn't come back, I'll have my baby. I'll do everything that I can to make it happy. It won't grow up with nobody, like I did."

"You told me your mother used to come and throw presents for you over the garden wall."

"She did, I think, but the other children made fun of her and I kind of pretended that she was nothing to do with me. I wish I hadn't done that now."

"They were jealous, Laurel, that's why. Who came with toys for them?"

She was right. Laurel regretted the way she'd behaved. She hoped her own child would never be ashamed of her.

"I was one of eleven. I was never special to anyone."

Next pay day, they went shopping and bought some big jumpers and jeans and an elastic girdle intended to ease the back ache of pregnant women. Wearing the smallest size kept the bump from being too obvious. Going back to school was out of the question. She knew she would be found out if she had to wear school uniform. Besides, it was great having money of her own. She stayed on at the children's home, waiting impatiently for her place at the hostel. Fid told Sean about the baby, but he kept Laurel's secret. He was so shy that he did not converse with many people besides Fid and his parents.

He knew his strict, religious parents would be outraged, so he kept silent.

# CHAPTER 4

## *December 1976*

Ben sat outside the hospital, waiting for Karen to emerge after her antenatal appointment. He spotted her well before she found the car. Her bump was so massive for her small frame that it looked like a giant Christmas pudding with legs attached. She was hurrying and seemed quite nimble despite her size. She saw him and waved excitedly, running as best she could with her burden.

"Guess what? We've got a date!" She threw herself, bottom first, into the little Hillman Imp.

"What do you mean? I mean, how could they know?"

"Because I've got to have a caesarean section and they've given me a date to go in! We know the baby's birthday already!"

"Why has that been decided?"

"It's because I've had an x-ray and the baby's too big for my pelvis. You've been looking after me too well with your healthy home cooking. We've grown a bouncing, bonny baby."

"Oh, I hope that's going to be ok!" Ben could not hide the concern in his voice.

"Of course it is, silly. At least now I don't have to go into labour and we can plan round it. We know the kid's birthday! It's so thrilling!" She grabbed Ben's neck and hugged him.

"Mm, I suppose so." Still not convinced, Ben started the car. They were going to the city centre, a few miles away from their town, to do some Christmas shopping. Karen was on maternity leave from the art college where they both worked. She had meant to do lots of things during this free time. Painting, sketching, doing up the attic in their flat, even perhaps some charity work was on the agenda. Instead, she found herself making baby things and falling asleep on the settee. Now the end was in sight, and scary as it was, it was also exciting.

They reached the shops, and bought presents for their colleagues and students at work. "We will have to get something to send for your mum and dad, Ben."

"Actually, I might be able to go down there, if it's ok with you. I had a call at work the other day. Do you remember Gary, he was in year three? Well, he's done very nicely with his work for television and he's asked me to go and do some designs for him. It will take a couple of days, that's all, but I didn't say yes because of you. If we know everything's alright so far, perhaps you could ask Molly to stay at ours while I'm away."

"Why didn't you say something before? It's a great idea. Your parents will be thrilled to see you and have you stay over."

"The pay's good too. It means we can finish converting the attic into a studio. It might lead to an opening. You never know," Ben said tentatively.

Karen was prone to wild optimism and he tried to play it down. But he'd been told that if it went well, there could be an interesting and lucrative job offer. He was happy with his job at the college, but more money would be welcome. They walked back to the car, chatting about babies' names, Ben's parents and the trip to London. On the way, they saw a group of people holding out leaflets to passers-by. Karen took one.

"Ben, it's about South Africa!" She rushed back to talk to the group, and soon became surrounded by them. Ben tried to call her back, but she disappeared into the crowd. Ben spent a few anxious minutes waiting for her. She was so small and ungainly she could easily be knocked and jostled. But she came out, flushed with enthusiasm. "Nelson Mandela's been in prison for eleven years now, for opposing the government and trying to get equality for his people. The group is carrying on his work. He's still changing things even in prison. Isn't that marvellous?"

"Yes, it's great to hear the work is still carrying on. Are they asking for money?"

"No, just awareness. I'd love to do that sort of thing."

"You will, just not at the moment." He put a protective arm around her as they set off back to the car.

# CHAPTER 5

The trio had a vague idea of what a baby might need, or at least Fidelma had. They stored a few things in a locked suitcase in Laurel's room. Saturdays out became scarcer as Laurel usually had to work that day. One precious Saturday off in December, Sean came to the cinema with a parcel for Laurel. Eagerly, she unwrapped it. It was a soft, downy teddy bear. She hugged it in delight.

Sean's shy features lit up at Laurel's pleasure. "Just thought of you when I saw it. It's for - er - you know who."

"Ooh, thanks, Sean! It's lovely!" Her eyes sparkled as she looked up at him. He blushed and beamed back at her. Fid took his hand and squeezed it, then the three friends entwined arms, united by their affection and their secret. They were to remember that happy moment for the rest of their lives.

The next day was Sunday, and the morning service was just as arduous as ever. Laurel found kneeling and rising more difficult than before, and her back was aching even when sitting still. As always, the church was cold and draughty. It hadn't bothered her as much since she became pregnant, but today she really felt it. However, she forgot about it as soon as she was back in her room and it didn't cross her mind again until Monday morning at work.

She climbed a small step ladder to reach a shelf and suddenly felt dizzy. She regained her balance almost immediately, but not before her supervisor spotted her staggering down. "What's up with you? Are you drunk?" She was joking, but there was a note of concern in her voice and she was staring at Laurel. "You ok?" she persisted when Laurel did not answer. "Come on, sit down for a minute." She led Laurel to a chair, still looking intently at her. "Come to the staff room for a little while."

"I'm alright, Brenda, honestly."

But Brenda took no notice of protestations and led

her up to the privacy of the staff room. Once there, Laurel flopped awkwardly into a chair and closed her eyes. When she opened them, Brenda said sadly, "Why didn't you tell me? We'll have to get you to a doctor. In fact, I'd better ring your social worker."

"Oh, please, I'm ok! I just felt a bit dizzy, that's all!"

Brenda had no medical training whatsoever but had no doubt what the problem was. She was annoyed with herself for not spotting it earlier. "I know you're having a baby, love. When did you last see the doctor?"

Laurel's voice was scarcely above a whisper. "No one knows. I've not been to the doctor's."

"Well, I'll have to ring your social worker, otherwise I'll be in trouble. But don't worry. We'll help you."

"I didn't want her to know. She'll make me give it away. I was thinking of running off."

"If you keep it you would be better off here with people you know. You'll need a lot of support. You've a better chance of keeping it if you've got friends to help."

"I've only got two friends. They both know."

Brenda's tone was gentle but she found it hard to keep the anxiety and concern out of her voice. The girl had no idea what was in front of her. She was a good worker and never complained or answered back. Brenda hated to think how hard it had been for her these last months, carrying on with no adult to confide in. She knew the teenage couple who came into the shop to meet her. They were sweet, but they weren't much older than Laurel.

The social worker arrived an hour later and was less sympathetic and not at all contrite, unlike Brenda. Miss Brown prided herself on her efficiency, and her well-cut hair, neat suit and polished court shoes reflected this image perfectly. Twenty years of social work had not softened her view of the carelessness of her charges' lives.

"Why didn't you say something, you silly girl?" She gave an exasperated sigh. "I can't believe you've let it go on to this stage without saying anything. When is it due, anyway?"

Laurel's childlike face looked up despondently. "I don't know, Miss Brown."

"Well when was your last period?"

"I don't know."

"You'll have to go straight to the doctor's. You have no right to keep this to yourself. I am responsible if anything happens to you. You're in my care."

Laurel let Miss Brown usher her out of the shop and followed meekly when she led her to the GP's. Brenda saw her off at the shop door. "Good luck! You'll be fine." Laurel smiled and waved gratefully.

Surgery was in progress and they had to wait to be seen. They sat in silence for nearly an hour. At last, it was her turn. The doctor examined her and addressed all his remarks to Miss Brown. "I'm afraid she will have to go to hospital today. The baby is at term and I think it's a breech presentation. She needs an x-ray to confirm this, but it can't wait. She could be in early labour. I'll give you a letter to take."

"Is everything alright?" Laurel's voice was hoarse with apprehension. It was beginning to sink in that this journey was unknown territory. She wished Fid was here, or even Brenda.

"Yes, everything's alright, but we need to go to hospital straightaway. My car's down the road."

During the drive, Miss Brown's annoyance began to melt. "Don't worry too much about the baby. We can soon find a nice family who would love to adopt a child. There's a shortage of coloured babies at the moment. I have a few African families who are desperate for a child."

"I want to keep it. I don't want to give it to someone else."

"How on earth can you manage a baby on your own at your age? I take it there's no sign of the father."

"He's in London at the moment, working. He'll be back soon."

"Will he, now! We'll see. But it's well known that that — er — these people have, shall we say, larger appetites

24

than — er — English people, indulge more often and can be unreliable. We can talk about that later. Right now we have to get you to a specialist. Once the baby's born we'll think again."

Laurel said nothing. There was no way this woman was going to get her hands on the baby.

The hospital staff were kind and reassuring. They explained everything to her without referring to Miss Brown, who interrupted constantly. She was to have an operation the next day and she was put to bed in a room with two other girls. At last Miss Brown left, promising to return with clothes and toiletries. Laurel sat nervously on the side of the bed, suddenly aware that she had no idea what was going to happen to her. The social worker was less than pleased with her, but even she was better than nothing.

"Hi, I'm Karen!"

She looked up and the girl sitting on the bed beside her was staring across at her. She was blonde and tiny, with long, flowing curls and bright blue eyes. Her belly was so round and large she looked as though she had hidden a beach ball under her nightie. She had a posh accent, similar to Miss Brown's. "Don't be scared. I'm having a section, too. So's Paula." She nodded across to the girl in the opposite bed. "There was a girl in that bed as well." She pointed to the one beside Paula. "They're leaving her till next week. She's furious!"

"What's a section?"

"It's an operation to get the baby out. It's what the doctor was talking about. Didn't you get it? It must have been hard to concentrate with that woman butting in all the time. Is she a neighbour or mother-in-law or something?"

"She's my social worker. She doesn't like me very much. I've had some nice ones in the past, but they've all left. I haven't got any relatives, just friends."

"Lucky you! Relatives aren't all they're cracked up to be. Especially fathers."

Laurel smiled uncertainly, unsure of what to say. Eyes downcast, she fiddled with the counterpane on her bed.

Karen immediately regretted her remarks. "Sorry, I'm so flippant at times. My father lives abroad and never bothers with me anymore. I'm sure there's lots of nice fathers around, but he's not one of them. My lovely husband's going to be a great father. So, who brought you up?"

"I live in a children's home. I'm waiting for my own place."

"Then we have something in common. I was packed off to boarding school when my mother died. It's like a children's home, only bigger. I even stayed there during the holidays, sometimes."

"Can you remember your mother?" Lauren asked.

"Yes, but it's a bit vague. I've got lots of pictures. Can you?"

"I can when I really try. Some people at the home had awful memories of their mothers, but mine are nice."

"My memories are nice, too," said Karen.

Lauren was beginning to relax a little. Karen seemed so friendly. "Didn't you like your father?" she ventured to ask.

"Well, he's alright, I suppose, but it's his wife who wears the trousers. She's something big in the civil service and I trod on a few toes as a teenager. I spoiled their wedding, actually."

Paula, who had not joined in the conversation until now, pricked up her ears. "How did you manage that?"

"Well, I'd come up from school for the wedding and the day before, there was a demonstration against the South African rugby team coming to England to play. Because of the apartheid, you know. Black people were treated really badly. Well, anyway, I went along and got arrested."

Both Laurel and Paula listened open-mouthed. It was hard to imagine that Karen, with her la-di-da accent and boarding school background was ever in trouble with the police.

"What the hell had you done?" gasped Paula.

"Oh, just lying down in the road when I was told to move on. Two policemen grabbed me and carried me to the police station. Because I was only sixteen they had to get my dad."

"I bet he was mad!" said Paula.

"He wasn't best pleased. But as long as *she* didn't find out, it wouldn't have been so bad. I told them I was going to be a bridesmaid the next day and they took pity on me and let me go with a caution. But there must have been a journalist around, because the day after the wedding I was on the front page of the Daily Standard."

"So you were famous!" Paula laughed.

"There were two pictures, one of me being carried off with a placard in my hands saying 'SPRINGBOK PISS OFF' over a drawing of two fingers doing the V sign, and wearing tatty old Levi's and a tie-dyed tee-shirt, and one with me at the wedding next day, all demure in high heels and an Ossie Clarke dress. I've still got the newspaper cutting. Needless to say, Dad's wife went mental!"

Paula and Karen started laughing, and despite her apprehension and awkwardness, Laurel joined in.

"I'm the boring one in this room," said Paula. "I've got two parents and a very ordinary husband. We've just bought our own house, a little terrace near the town centre. I'm having twins and they're in each other's way so I need a caesarean section. That's the most interesting thing about me."

"We've just bought somewhere, too. I got some money from my father when I was twenty-one, so we used it for a top-storey flat in a big old house. It's perfect for my husband's work. He's an artist. We both teach art, but he is really talented. He's away in London at the moment, having an exhibition."

"My boyfriend's in London too," said Laurel.

"Does he know you're in here?" Karen tried to keep the question casual.

27

"Er, no, he doesn't." She did not want to give any more information and to avoid an awkward moment, Karen said quickly, "My husband doesn't know, either. My section should have been next week, but my waters broke this morning."

Laurel looked mystified. "I'm not sure what that means."

"Didn't you go to antenatal classes?" Paula asked. "They tell you all about that sort of thing."

"No, I didn't tell anyone, except two friends, Fidelma and Sean. Until today."

Karen smiled reassuringly. "I went to classes regularly. They told me all about labour, but I won't be going into labour and neither will either of you. So you've not missed much, Laurel."

"Does your father know about the baby?" Paula asked Karen.

"He doesn't even know I'm married. We lost contact after I got arrested again."

"Again!" Paula's eyes were wide with amazement.

"Well it was during the miners' strike. I was on the picket line and somehow, by accident I managed to knock a policeman's helmet off. Because of his very important wife, I think I was a bit of a security risk. So two years later, when I was twenty-one, he sent me the money and I've never heard from him since. It was her or me, I think."

Laurel was fascinated. She had always imagined that people with money and background lived a charmed life without problems. Karen looked across at her. "Life's not all roses for me, either," she said, interpreting Laurel's expression. "But I've had a better deal than you." She smiled kindly and gave a reassuring wink.

They were silent for a few moments. Laurel felt that she could trust these two women. "I'm going to keep my baby. I'm not going to let the social worker get her hands on it. That's why I never told anybody. If I had, they'd be planning it already."

"Good for you!" Paula grinned across to her.

"We'll help. We can come and see you," said Karen.

A nurse came in at that moment. "A note for you." She handed Laurel a scrap of paper. It read: *They won't let us in because visiting's finished now. Can we bring you anything tomorrow? Love Fid and Sean x*

Laurel wrote on the back: *Bossy Brown wants to give the baby to some African couple she knows. Over my dead body!! It stays with me! Fetch the baby case, some Toffos and a bar of Turkish Delight. Love Laurel xx.*

She gave the note back. "My two friends," she explained to Paula and Karen.

"Ok, girls. Lights out. Big day tomorrow." The nurse left with Laurel's note and meekly they all settled down to sleep.

A few minutes later, Laurel heard Karen whisper to Paula. "Has she gone off?"

"I think so."

"Poor cow. I could have hit that bloody social worker. I'm going to keep in touch. She needs someone on her side. I don't think the father's willing to do much, reading between the lines. He's already done his bit, I'll bet."

"You're right. She needs help. But my mum was only a teenager when she had me, and I turned out ok."

Laurel kept quiet, pretending to be asleep, but inside she was rejoicing. She now had two more friends who did not want to take her baby from her. It didn't seem so scary after all.

# CHAPTER 6

Clara came to work that morning on just an ordinary day. She fought with the same person for a parking space, got irritated when she changed into her uniform and found the laundry had shrunk her dress again, and put her sandwiches in the fridge on the back shelf so that no one would steal them.

Her assignment was to look after three patients, all having caesarean sections before lunch. They were all in the four-bedded ward next to the theatre, so that they would be close to both theatre staff and ward staff. The first on the list was a twenty-two-year-old with twins, the next was being operated on because of her small pelvis, and the third was a sixteen-year-old with a baby in the breech position. All three came back from the theatre without any complications. It was Clara's job to give them morphine for pain relief, monitor their progress and look after the babies.

The theatre staff had a little sitting room near the double doors at the entrance. After the last patient left, they relaxed in there for a short cigarette break and a gossip before clearing up.

"Did you see 'The Sweeny' last night?" Phil, the anaesthetist asked Shelley, the theatre sister.

"No, was it any good?"

"Dunno. I didn't watch it either. I just wanted to know if you went out or not. That new houseman wasn't around either. Is there something going on between you two?"

He was leaning back in his chair, so without answering she pushed him backwards so that he fell off. "Charming!" He got up, pretending to be annoyed. "I think the violence proves it."

Her reply was a derisive snort.

"I don't know what you see in him, when I'm available."

"Shall I make a list?"

"Ah! I knew you fancied him!"

"I didn't say I fancied him!"

"No need! It's written all over your face!"

The conversation caught the interest of the rest of the staff and nobody noticed that Phil's cigarette had fallen into the bin at his side. A few minutes later, he felt something warm around his ankles.

"My god, the bin's on fire!"

"You and your fags! You're such a nuisance! What an idiot!" Shelley admonished him.

Phil jumped up to extinguish the flames, but somehow he knocked the bin over and it rolled across the little room. There was a pile of paper in the corner, discarded there after being used to wrap the sterile packs of instruments. Instantly they set alight. Phil rushed to the door and stamped on them, but in the process, overturned a large rack of paper packs in the theatre doorway. The shelving unit fell against the double doors of the theatre suite, blocking their exit and setting fire to the rubber mattresses and cotton blankets on the trolleys positioned in the porch. Almost before they could take it in, the theatre entrance was ablaze. There was a door in the theatre's sluice room which led straight outside, with a metal spiral staircase to the yard at the back of the building. There was nowhere else to go. Shelley immediately took charge, pressed the alarm bell and gathered her staff together and got them down the fire escape and safely out of the building and onto the ground.

Smoke was now billowing out of the theatre into the main corridor. Clara smelled the smoke before she saw it through the glass wall of the four-bedded ward. Seconds later, the fire bell screamed stridently into the ward. The three mothers slept on, but Clara could hear the other patients scurrying out of their beds into the corridor. For a few moments, Clara froze, unable to move. Terror made her stomach leap into her throat. She couldn't get the sleeping women out on her own. She tried to wake them, even though she knew they wouldn't be able to walk after the sedatives she'd given them and the anaesthetic that was still in their system. They all moved and groaned, but that was all the response she could get. She looked helplessly at their sleeping forms.

But then she realised she could take the babies. She picked them up and placed them all in one cot. The twin boys snuggled down next to each other, but Laurel's and Karen's babies, both girls, wriggled and cried in the confined space. Then she made for the door. The cot was a large basin affair sitting on a cupboard with castors. It was normally quite easy to manoeuvre, but fear made her clumsy and she banged it several times against the door frame. At last she got through and turned to see Paula struggling to get out of bed. Her arm had a drip needle in it, attached to a tube leading to a bag of fluid hooked on to a drip-stand on wheels. That, and her drugged and weak body prevented her from standing up. Clara took a precious few seconds to help her up. Then they began the journey down the long corridor to the ward exit. Paula clung to the drip stand for support, pushing it along in front of her. The smoke billowing out of the open theatre doors clouded their vision, and though they could hear other people ahead of them they couldn't see them and could barely see each other.

The sound of a fire engine's siren, muffled and distorted, pierced Clara's consciousness for a few seconds, but her mind was on her destination. The lift shaft was positioned half way down the corridor. They managed to get there, only to find the doors had closed automatically when the fire bell was activated. Clara wanted to scream, but somehow managed to stifle it and gather her thoughts for long enough to carry on. There was an exit farther on. They had to get there.

Paula was staggering now, but her instinct to follow her babies was strong enough to keep her going. The whole experience felt like a strange nightmare. Her woolly brain could only partly comprehend what was happening. The drugs Paula had floating around in her system dulled the pain but increased the feeling of unreality. Clara's eyes were streaming and her nose and throat were burning as they carried on down the corridor. There was a strange sensation in her stomach as it churned over and over. It was hard to gather any rational thoughts. All she could concentrate on was getting out. They could no longer hear anyone else in front of them. By this time, they had no idea of time or place or how far away from the exit they were. Clara realised that every sensation, every sight, smell and feeling was heightened. She recognised this acute awareness. It was fear. Somehow she rose above it enough to carry on.

At last they made it to the fire doors leading to a stone staircase to the emergency exit. With a great effort, Clara succeeded in pushing open the door with her body and unhooked Paula's bag of fluid from the drip stand and threaded it onto Paula's finger. A rush of cold air soothed her nose and throat. Then she lifted the boxful of babies from its stand and set off down the stairs, feeling for each step as she went. She could hear voices as she approached the outer door. Then at last, she was there, forcing it open with her weight. A quick glance behind her revealed Paula, crawling now and clinging to the stair rail, a trail of blood in her wake. Someone took Clara's precious burden from her and her legs suddenly gave way and she fainted.

She came round a few minutes later to find that Phil, the anaesthetist she had squabbled with over a parking space that morning was giving her oxygen from an emergency cylinder they hadn't used for years. The surgeon who had operated on Paula three hours earlier was crying whilst carrying her in his arms. The courtyard was full of women with babies and some porters were running across the car park with incubators.

"Two girls!" She thought she was shouting the words, but it came out as a hoarse whisper. Then she lost consciousness again.

Meanwhile, Laurel and Karen, floating above their bodies in a drug-fuelled haze, slept peacefully on, unaware in their morphine dreams of the commotion going on around them.

# CHAPTER 7

Paula lived. She lived, despite blood loss, dehydration, lung damage and superficial burns to her hands caused by gripping the metal drip stand. The girl who should have occupied the fourth bed in the ward would be forever mindful of her lucky postponement of her admission. Her family talked about it for years. It was two days before Christmas. Everyone who could possibly be discharged was sent home. The maternity unit closed its doors and sent away the remaining patients to hospitals in the next town. Paula and her twin boys shared an uncomfortable ambulance journey to spend three weeks in a hospital ten miles away, but got home to have a loving childhood with two parents and an extended family.

Laurel and Karen's little girls were kept in different special care baby units in the area until they recovered from smoke inhalation.

The tragedy shocked the whole town. Christmas became a much quieter celebration. The funerals could not be arranged until the festivities were over. Even the post mortems were delayed.

Fid and Sean found it hard to understand. It wasn't real. Fid would wake up thinking she had dreamt it all. Sean wanted to wave at Laurel's window every time he passed. The day of her funeral was cold, bright and frosty. Father Michael's church had never been so well attended. The old, draughty building was warmed by the extraordinarily large numbers of humans inside. The community who ignored her in life, came together to mourn her in death. The schoolmates she felt so different from came to show the respect they had never afforded her when she needed it.

The choirboys who would normally spend free time doing wheelies on their chopper bikes, attended every rehearsal and sang like angels. The nuns prayed for her and the children and staff from the home were present to a man. The firemen who had carried Laurel and Karen out of the ward window and tried desperately to revive them, turned up in full uniform. Only Carl was absent.

Fid and Sean sat at the back of the church, with Sean's parents, bewildered by all the strange faces. It was a long ceremony. Many people lined up for communion, a sure sign of the insecurity the accident had generated. Half the day passed before the party left for the graveside. People stood shivering around the grave only half listening to Father Michael's words. The staff from the children's home provided food for the mourners, and gradually, everyone drifted off in that direction. Fid and Sean were the last to leave the cemetery. Father Michael, who had observed Fid and Laurel's friendship since it started, took Fid's hands in his. He didn't attempt to say any comforting words, but simply smiled into her eyes. She stared back at him, desolate and confused. He turned to Sean. "Look after her."

"I'll do my best," Sean promised.

Father Michael nodded and went on his way. Fid and Sean held hands and started to leave.

"Just a minute!" It was Miss Brown. "Could I speak to you? I know it's not the best time, but you were her closest friends. Can you tell me anything about the father? I need to arrange an adoption, if possible."

Fid's brain could not form an answer, but Sean said, "He went to London in the summer and we haven't seen him since. He didn't know about the baby."

"Well, if I'm placing it, I need to know what he looks like, how tall he is, how dark he is, and so on. Unfortunately, we won't have much else to go on."

"He's small, with blonde hair and he's clever. That's all I can think of."

"Heavens, you mean he's white? He's English? I had a family in mind, but... I must go and see the baby. It may be difficult to place."

"She. It's a girl." Fid spoke for the first time. Her voice was soft and polite, but there was resentment there which

36

she could not hide.

"Yes, of course." Miss Brown was slightly embarrassed that Fid had corrected her. "It must be a very difficult time for you. I'm so sorry."

With that, she hurried off.

"She couldn't care less." Said Fid through clenched teeth. "Laurel didn't want Bossy Brown interfering. It's the last thing she wanted."

"I wish we knew where Carl is," Sean answered. "Do you think he'll come back?"

"I don't think he meant to come back in the first place. I realise that now."

"Yes, I think you're right." Sean said carefully, trying not to upset Fid any further.

"Sean, I don't want to go back to the home just yet, I can't face all those people."

"It's alright. Come home with me and I'll make us a cup of tea. Then I'll walk you back when they've all gone."

Fid held his hand tighter and nuzzled her face into the crook of his arm. Sean stroked her hair with his free hand, relieved that he had managed to comfort her.

# CHAPTER 8

A few days later, Fid and Sean made the journey to the next town where Laurel's baby was being looked after. She was in an incubator. It was the first time Sean had seen a baby so new. Her face was slightly wrinkly and her skin was still a dusky pink. Only her navy blue eyes and her light brown fingertips gave her ethnicity away.

One of the nurses came over to speak to them. "I'm the person looking after baby Laura. Are you relatives?"

"No, but close friends. Laurel had no relatives. We are all she had."

"Well, in that case I can speak to you about her. She'll be in hospital for some time. There is some lung damage, but we are hoping that it will repair itself. She needs oxygen at the moment, but as soon as she improves, we can put her in a cot and then you will be able to hold her."

"That would be wonderful!" Fid was thrilled at the thought.

The nurse smiled kindly. "The social worker is looking for a placement for her. There is some delay in finding suitable adoptive parents because of the health and also the mixed race issues."

Fid and Sean stared into the glass box, fascinated by what they saw. "How dark blue those eyes are!" said Fid.

"They won't stay like that. Most babies are born with blue eyes, but dark eyes usually turn brown after a time."

They stayed to watch Laura's nappy change and bottle feed. "This is the first day she's been bottle fed." The nurse explained. "We were tube feeding her until this morning."

"How come she's called Laura?" Fid asked.

"It was the closest we could think of to her mother's name. Normally when the parents don't choose a name, the baby's called the same as the parent, but it didn't seem right in this case. There's no relatives at all to ask. Had mum chosen a name for her?"

"No, she was going to wait until after the birth."

"Well, I hope she'd be ok with Laura."

Fid smiled shyly. The nurse seemed really nice. "I'm sure she'd be happy with Laura. It's a good name."

On the bus journey home, a thought occurred to Fid. "What if, as they can't find anybody, we asked if we could adopt? I know Laurel would like that."

Sean was silent for a moment. The baby was lovely, but as an only child, he knew nothing about looking after one. But Fid did. And it would be the next best thing to Laurel. "It's a great idea. You'd have to move into mam and da's with her. We'd need to get married. But I'd love that, Fid. We'd be a family."

Together, during the hour-long bus ride, they planned their life together and imagined watching Laura change and grow. By the time they were home, they had mentally redecorated the spare room at Sean's, prepared a speech for the social worker and altered Fid's working hours to fit in with child care.

The first step was to see Miss Brown. Fid arranged an appointment. She wore her best clothes and Sean put on his father's old suit, which was what he wore for any occasion except work. The social workers had a small office in the children's home, which was used from time to time to interview parents, or children. Fid cleaned that room every week, but had never been involved in its use before. It was a strange sensation to be sitting in it.

"Well, how can I help?" Miss Brown said briskly. "I assume you know a bit more about the baby's father? Has he turned up? Is that why you want me?" She looked expectantly into their eager faces.

There was a short silence before Fid said, "We haven't seen him since last summer. We've come to see if we can adopt the baby. The hospital said you haven't found anybody yet and..."

"Let me stop you there! Adoption isn't a baby sale and infants aren't given away like Christmas presents. Adoptive parents are subject to rigorous scrutiny and there is a very strict criteria. Every miniscule detail of their lives is examined."

"We have somewhere to live and we both have jobs. I come from a big family so I know all about babies."

Miss Brown gave a condescending smile. "I'm sure you do, but it takes a great deal more than that to satisfy the board at Children's Services. For a start, you're not even married. That puts a child at the risk of a breakup."

"We can get married. We've always known we would. We've been together since primary school."

"Yes but you're also very young."

"We're both nineteen next week. My mother was nineteen when she had her first baby."

Miss Brown sighed patiently and spoke patronisingly clearly and slowly. "I'm afraid it's not possible. It would be unfair to process your application when I know that you don't fulfil even the basics of the criteria. But thank you very much for your interest."

They were dismissed. They got up to go. Sean had not said a word during the whole interview.

"I'm so sorry." It was an afterthought as they closed the door.

In silence, they walked back to Sean's parents' house. The parents were away at a social event with the church club.

"Shall I put the kettle on?" Sean asked tentatively as Fid sat, defeated and dejected at the kitchen table.

"Is that all you've got to say? Shall I put the kettle on? You didn't say a word in there, you great lummox. I may as well have had a sack of spuds sat next to me. Why are you so bloody useless? Why can't you make some effort for once, instead of letting that prissy old cow walk all over us?"

"What could I have said?"

"We'll never bloody know now, will we? On second thoughts, it's probably a good job you kept your gob shut. You'd have made things worse, if they could have got any worse."

"Ok, I'm useless. I can't even be trusted to make the

40

tea! See?"

He grabbed a mug tree from the shelf and flung it onto the stone floor. Fid gave him a withering look and got up to survey the damage. Two mugs were still intact so she placed them on the table. Then she picked up a broom and began furiously sweeping up the debris. As soon as there was a clear space, Sean picked up the two whole mugs in his huge fist and smashed them. Bits of china flew into the air and scattered around the kitchen. Fid threw down the broom and sat with her back to Sean, arms folded and shoulders rigid.

Sean's anger was draining away as quickly as it had risen. He stared at Fid's defiant back view. "I had nothing to add, Fid. I can't make people do things. I didn't know all those big words anyway." No answer but a stiffening of the neck. There was silence for a few minutes. He tried again. "I loved Laurel too, Fid. Not like you loved her, and not like I love you. But I still loved her. I thought we'd hold the baby, and take her out with Laurel. She would want us to have the baby. But no one listens to me. I know that."

Fid didn't turn round, but her head slowly dropped forward and her shoulders drooped. Sean went across and put a nervous arm around her, still unsure of her reaction. But the fight had gone out of her and she sank into his embrace. "Oh, Sean, I so wanted that baby. She never even took us seriously. We're as good as any of those posh people who come to the children's home for babies."

"We know we are. That's what matters."

He pulled her towards him and they kissed and clung to each other. He caressed her breasts and buttocks under her clothing. Usually, she only tolerated this for a short time, then the guilt of a good catholic girl took over and she would push him away. But today she melted into his arms and allowed him to explore her body, first with his hands and then with his mouth. Soon, he was inside her and they were making love under the table. Their grief, frustrations and disappointments found an outlet and for

41

a brief time there was nothing but their passion and each other.

Afterwards, Fid lay on her back next to Sean, staring at the underside of the pine table. Sharp shards of china were pricking at her legs. She began to feel a bit silly. Although the front of her body was naked, she still had her coat on. The cold of the stone floor was beginning to penetrate. She was wearing one shoe and the other one was nowhere to be seen. It wasn't quite the seduction she'd dreamed of. Real life wasn't like the films after all.

# CHAPTER 9

They vowed not to do it again. But, of course, they did. The closeness, the freedom from inhibition and the shared intimacy were things that they badly needed at that time. They were not used to keeping secrets and this, plus the limitation of their opportunities made sex even more special. Although they had always loved each other, they were never in love. Until now. Fid never felt the earth move, the stars were no brighter than before, and Sean didn't turn into a prince. He remained just Sean. But she was in love, and so was he.

The young gardeners who worked alongside Sean and his father in the local parks discussed their conquests all the time. Sean was teased constantly about his relationship with Fid. The presence of his father and his natural reticence helped him keep his secret.

"Hey, Brendan!" said Tom, a cheeky twenty-year-old who was a hit with girls. "Why don't you let your lad out with us? He's a big boy now. It's about time he got his end away. We can fix him up with a goer."

"Mr Flanagan to you lot. He's going nowhere. He's got a lovely girlfriend."

"But she's not doing him much good, is she?"

"She's a well-brought-up young lady, so she is, and don't you lot say a word against her to me. She's like a daughter to me already."

"Ooh, sorry I spoke!" Tom winked at his workmates. Winding up Brendan was a perk of the job.

Sean's guilty conscience turned his face from off-white to puce and every shade in between, but this didn't betray him. They all knew that he hated being talked about and looked no further for the cause of his embarrassment. So far, so good.

The snowdrops died off and the crocuses and primroses raised their heads. Mornings became lighter and new-born lambs appeared in the fields. And, inevitably, Mother Nature had one more trick up her sleeve. Sean was much less adept at contraception than his workmates and soon, Fid realised she was pregnant.

"Oh, God, what can I say to your mother?" Fid's first thought was of the embarrassment it would cause Sean's strict, God-fearing family.

"Oh, don't worry about her. It's straight to the church she'll be, to pray for us sinners."

"I didn't want a rushed wedding. I wanted to save up and plan it. Especially as we're not allowed baby Laura. We could have taken our time."

"We'll have our own baby, Fid. No one can tell us we're too young or too poor."

"You're right, Sean. People will get used to it."

And they did. Sean's mother took part of the guilt on herself. "Fidelma Murphy, what will your mother think of me? Bridie, she said to me when we set sail for England, 'Look after my little girl'. I will, I said, like she's my own daughter. You're as near as I'll ever get."

"I'm sorry, Bridie. I didn't mean to let you down. It sort of just happened. Will you not let Mam know till I've told her?"

"Well, you'd better be quick. I write Kathleen every two weeks and if she doesn't get a letter she'll know something's up. I've kept nothing from her since we were at school together." Bridie's thin face shadowed over with anxiety at the thought of deceiving her best friend. She was ashamed of her son. He was brought up better than this. But, although she didn't say so, the baby was welcome.

Sean's father, like his son, was a man of few words. "She's no better than she should be, and neither are you. You'll be needing the spare room, I suppose," he added grudgingly.

The spare room was Brendan's hideout, where he listened to the radio, read the sports pages and tinkered with bits of metal and a soldering iron. It was the one place in the house where he could spread his huge frame without getting in anyone's way. Giving it up would be a great sacrifice, even though their third bedroom was only six-foot square.

"I'll build you a shed, Da, to be sure I will," Sean tried to appease him. A grunt was the only response but it was enough to reassure Sean that he and Fid would have some support.

It was a small wedding. Fid's family could not arrange to get across to England for several weeks, so the couple planned to visit Ireland in the summer for a celebration there. Brendan provided spring flowers for Father Michael to decorate the church and two little girls from the children's home were bridesmaids. Fid wore a white dress and Sean was prised out of his comfort clothes and into a borrowed suit for the occasion. It wasn't the wedding Fid had imagined, but nonetheless, she was happy to be by Sean's side.

Their honeymoon was two nights in a hotel in a pretty village a few miles away. "Fidelma Flanagan! What a mouthful!" she laughed as she signed the hotel register. "I should have made you change your name!"

Brendan and Bridie had decorated Sean's room and made matching curtains and bed linen to welcome them home. All four made efforts to settle down together and adjust to the new life. Sean's parents were secretly looking forward to the new baby, even though they disapproved of its untimely conception.

Then, a few weeks after the wedding, Fid was squatting to clean behind a cupboard in the girls' dormitory when she noticed a red stain in the crotch of her jeans. At first, she was puzzled, then gave a gasp of dismay as she realised what it meant. It was rapidly growing larger. She had told no one at work that she was pregnant. They may have guessed, but no one had mentioned it. She certainly didn't want to discuss it now. Hastily, she put her coat on and made some excuse about a bad headache and walked home, through the park where Brendan and Sean worked. It was a lovely spring day. The sun shone for the first time for weeks. The daffodils her husband had planted nodded graciously at her in the breeze and the twigs on the trees were filled with tiny buds like beads on a necklace. But Fid was aware of nothing but the black cloud obscuring everything else in her world. Sean tried his best to reassure her on the way to the doctor's, telling her it would all be alright and it probably happened to pregnant women all the time. She was aware that he knew nothing about such matters and also that he felt awkward speaking of such things, but she didn't argue. Instead, she smiled at him and nodded.

It was all over by bedtime. Her doctor sent her to hospital and she was discharged the following evening. Brendan came for her in his works van. Neither of them spoke. The noise of the tired old engine and the rattling of the spades and rakes in the back did nothing to dispel the awkward silence.

They reached home and Sean carried her to bed, where she curled up and cried herself to sleep. She awoke next morning with nothing to get up for. "Yesterday, I had a future. I've lost Laurel, Laura, and now my baby."

She realised she'd said the words aloud when Sean said, "You've still got me, Fid."

She tried to smile. "Yes I've still got you, Sean."

# CHAPTER 10

Bridie and Fid were sitting at the kitchen table, sharing a cup of tea and a potato cake. "Eat your breakfast, girl. Keep your strength up." Bridie peered anxiously into Fid's face. Although Bridie was tall and slim, she looked like an Amazon in comparison to Fid, whose frame seemed to have shrunk with the grief she was carrying. Her sad eyes seemed larger and greener than ever. "I made those especially for you. If the men come in, there'll be none left in no time at all."

Fid gave a sad little smile. "It's very kind you are, Bridie, but I'm not hungry. Perhaps I'll have something later."

"Fid, I had lots of miscarriages before I got Sean, and quite a few after. You've just got to keep trying."

"Sure it's hard when everywhere I go there's women with babies."

"Sure and don't I know how that feels, with your mother having a child every year and her my best friend? Praise God I got there in the end. Not that it will take you as long," she added hastily. "Anyway, it's only a week gone. Too early yet to start again. I always waited till my next period."

Bridie had never talked about such personal things before, and Fid was touched. But it didn't help. Maybe going back to the normal routine was what she needed. At least that's what everyone else thought.

She had said nothing at work, blaming her absence on a bout of flu. She didn't feel up to coping with the sympathy. After a week's sick leave she was back, cleaning the rooms as usual, pretending she still had a life. Sean stood by patiently at home, having no idea what to do or say.

The weeks went by, and the trees in the park began to blossom and the grass grew thicker and greener under Brendan's and Sean's care. Gradually, Fid took an interest in life again. There was music to listen to, church dances to go to, window shopping to do, clothes to buy. They were all things she would have done with Laurel, but somehow she managed to do them without her. Laurel loved dancing and that was one of the things Fid missed most. Sean could not get his large, muscular frame to do anything as precise as dancing and he was forbidden to try anything so embarrassing in public. But somehow, Fid's life went on, and the Flanagans settled down to wait for another pregnancy, and although the silence on the subject was almost tangible at times, the whole family was on alert.

Spring turned to summer. Brendan and Sean and their little team were busy mowing lawns, pruning bushes and uprooting weeds. The park became a lush green haven, filled with flowers. The rose garden was beautiful that year, ablaze with sweet-smelling varieties in pink, red white and yellow. It was a sunny, warm summer. Though the earth was fertile, Fid was not so lucky.

The trip to Ireland was a great success. Although Fid had been dreading the remarks she knew she would endure from the family and the rest of the village, she coped with them somehow. The Murphy house was festooned with ribbons saying "Welcome home!" and "Congratulations!" All her brothers and sisters and their offspring crowded into the modest house and garden and everyone brought home cooked food. Drink flowed freely and the party went on for two days. Even the local priest, who had christened both Fid and Sean, turned up to welcome them back. Her mother and her friends regaled Fid with dozens of old wives' tales about getting pregnant, but she kept as cool as she could.

All too soon it was time to go. The long journey by ferry and then by Brendan's old van upset Fid and she was feeling dreadful by the time she got home. Nothing was said, but Sean, Bridie and even Brendan were quietly hopeful. However, next day she got her period, and although she never mentioned it, they knew.

Back at work, the staff were pleased to see Fid. There was some news. "Guess what?" One of the carers came up to her as she was cleaning the dining room. "That Brown woman's been promoted. She's leaving for a better job and more money. I'll bet it's the only way to get rid of her."

"God, I'm not sorry to see the back of the old trout! When's she going?" Fid asked.

"Already gone and tied up all her work here and passed it on to a new social worker. The new one's introduced herself to us. She seems nice. She wants to see you as well."

Fid was horrified. "Holy Mother of God! What does she want to see me for? The room's clean enough. I did it before I left on holiday."

"Dunno," the carer answered. "I think it's just to say 'Hi' so that when she turns up for the children we'll know her. She's here now. You won't recognise Brownie's old office. Just knock on."

In Miss Brown's day, entering that office was by appointment only. Apart from the one disappointing time, Fid had never been in there except to clean. Hesitantly, she approached the door and gave an apprehensive tap.

"Come in!" a cheerful voice called out. The person behind the desk was slightly overweight, in her forties and dressed in jeans and a pretty top. Her mousy hair was pulled into an untidy ponytail, wisps of which were escaping onto her forehead. She wore no makeup. Fid was taken aback. She was as unlike her predecessor as it was possible to be. There were a few welcome changes to the room, which had been brightened up with flowers and pictures, but the most noticeable was the friendly atmosphere. "I'm Angela. We've not met before, have we? Are you one of the carers?"

"No, I'm the cleaner."

"Ah, you must be Fidelma. I'm so pleased to meet you." She held out a careworn hand. There was an old wedding ring on her finger, worn thin like Bridie's. "There's something I want to put to you. You were very close to Laurel Briggs, weren't you? I believe you were great friends."

Fid nodded, unsure where this was leading.

"I was reading the notes on baby Laura. I must tell you that she is not up for adoption at the moment. There are some medical problems which require her to be monitored at the hospital for some time. I thought you might like to know."

"She may not go to parents as there is also a difficulty in finding a family with the right ethnic background, as there's no relatives and you and your husband are the only ones who visited. There is no next of kin. Miss Brown assumed that her mother would give consent to adoption, but nothing was signed. Legally, she is the responsibility of Social Services. It's probable that she will spend her childhood in care. I'd like her to have some family, someone who knew her real parents, people she feels she belongs to. I'm asking if you would like contact with her. It's highly irregular, but it's not illegal. We don't know if that may be all she has, besides foster parents."

"Yes, I'd like that." Fidelma blushed to the roots of her red hair. She could hardly believe what she was hearing.

Angela smiled at Fid's obvious pleasure. "I cannot guarantee that things will not change in the future and that Laura may be moved away. The best interests of the child should be considered above everything else. But for some time she will be living in a place where all the other children have visitors from time to time. I don't want her to stand out as unwanted."

"We'll be glad to," said Fid. It had occurred to her that there may be more heartache if they were forced to lose contact but she didn't care. It might be worth it. This woman had given her part of Laurel back.

"I wonder," Angela went on, "have you thought of doing any other job besides cleaning? You seem very young to have settled for this."

"It's all they had when I came to England. I don't have

any qualifications and there was no work in my village."

"You're still young enough to get some training. Oh, I'm sorry, it's none of my business, of course." She realised she had been too forthright. "I've got teenagers of my own, and I tend to be a bit too bossy. I didn't mean to interfere."

"I don't know how to go about it, but I've always wanted to be a hairdresser. I'd like to take a beauty course. I'd enjoy making people look nice. But we need my wages."

Angela smiled. "I could show you how to apply for a part-time course. I've done it for some of the children in my care." Fid was overwhelmed. This person was really good. She was opening up a new world. "Oh and before I forget, I have something I'd like to give to you for safekeeping," Angela said as she pulled a battered old case from a cupboard. "This rightly belongs to Laura as her mother's next of kin, so if you could put it away somewhere for her? If it stays here and the staff change, no one will know what it's for."

Fid opened the case. On top was the soft teddy Sean had bought the week before Laurel died. Beside it, peeking out amongst some baby vests and nappies, was a framed photograph of the four of them at Belle Vue. Unable to speak, Fid hugged the teddy, her tears falling into the silky fur.

A few weeks later, a formal letter arrived to tell Fid she could visit Laura every Sunday at her children's home. Laura was to be placed with staff who were used to dealing with children with medical problems. Angela had included an application form for a part time course at the local college, and a hand-written note attached to say that she could organise her working hours around the lectures. Life was getting better.

# CHAPTER 11

## *July 1982*

Laura could not remember a time when she did not know Auntie Fid and Uncle Sean. It seemed they had been coming to visit her and that she had been visiting them for ever. Every Sunday she went to their house. Every Wednesday she went to the hospital with Auntie Barbara and the two other children who lived with them. The others were quite poorly, so Laura was always the first out, sitting in the waiting room until the others had been seen.

She didn't mind going to see the doctors and nurses. They were nice and always gave her a sticker which said 'I've been good at the doctor's'. Before she could read, Auntie Barbara would read it to her. However, it always said the same thing. Wednesdays were good, but Sunday was her favourite day. She would be taken there at dinner time, just as Gran Bridie was cooking a chicken. The kitchen smelled good and made her feel hungry. After they had eaten, Uncle Sean would sit her on his knee and read stories. There was a garden in the back and he would tell her all about the plants. She had put some seeds into pots and every week they checked together to see if they'd grown. Auntie Fid brushed her hair, saying "What lovely black curls." Auntie Fid's hair was straight and red.

Sometimes they went to the park to play on the swings and roundabouts. There were cakes and jelly at tea time, and after tea Auntie Fid would bathe her and put her pyjamas on. Then Grandad Brendan would drive her back in his van. She always pretended to be asleep when she was near home, because she knew that Grandad Brendan would carry her into the house and Auntie Barbara would put her straight to bed.

But today was different. Auntie Barbara got her up much earlier and they set off as soon as breakfast was over. "We're going to the seaside today," Auntie Fid said, smiling at her. "It's a lovely day. Look, the sun's shining. You can take your bucket and spade, so you can."

"What for?" Laura asked, curiously.

Auntie Fid came to the rescue. "There's lots of sand to make sandcastles, and you'll see the sea. Me and Sean will show you."

"I've never seen the sea." This was exciting.

"Sure, it's just like the pictures in the story books that Uncle Sean shows you. Or like the telly. But it's better when it's real."

"Ooh great!" Laura ran round in a little circle, delighted at the thought.

"You'd better be a good girl, mind. And do everything you're told," warned Auntie Fid.

"Oh I will, honest!"

Auntie Fid smiled. She was always smiling.

The journey seemed very long to Laura. They went in the van, with Uncle Sean driving and the rest of the family sitting in the back, except for Grandad Brendan. He had taken all his tools out make room. He stayed at home to do some odd jobs. It was a bumpy ride and she was beginning to feel a bit queasy when at last the van stopped and they could get out. But as soon as Uncle Sean opened the door, the air felt different.

"What's that smell?" Laura asked.

"It's the sea, Laura. Doesn't it smell good?" And Fid smiled down at her, eyes all crinkly at the corners. The walk from the car to the beach seemed a long one to Laura's little legs. However, there were lots of strange, interesting things to look at on the way. Shops selling fluffy pink clouds on sticks, people wearing huge hats and horses and carriages like Cinderella's coach were just a few. It was hard to take it all in.

At last, they went down some stone steps. At the bottom, she saw sand, stretching out on all sides of her, way bigger than any sand pit she had ever seen. Laura saw lots of people on the beach, so she was surprised to hear

Auntie Fid say, "Oh good, it's not too crowded. Let's find a spot to sit down."

Gran Bridie spread a blanket on the sand and they all sat on it. There was roast chicken to eat and sandwiches, apple and cake. There was even some fizzy lemonade. Uncle Sean showed her how to make a sandcastle, then Auntie Fid took her to paddle in the sea. It was another long walk. There were shells and seaweed on the way, and sometimes the sand was soft and squidgy and poked up between her toes if she pressed too hard. The waves washed her feet clean when she came to them. The sun shone on the water and turned it into an array of big flashy jewels like the ones Auntie Barbara wore. She got so excited she had to run around, splashing in and out of the waves. Bits of foam collected at the water's edge and Laura stood in it for a few seconds, letting the bubbles tickle her toes. They were there for a long time. She was happy by the water and didn't want to go back yet. But Aunty Fid saw an ice cream van.

"What about a 99? What do you think about that, Laura?"

"What's a ninety-nine?"

Aunty Fid pointed to a picture on the side of the van. It showed a cornet with a chocolate stick in the top. It looked delicious.

Laura let herself be led away and they stood together in the queue. After a few minutes, Laura got bored and wandered a few feet from Aunty Fid to pick up shells. There were lots of different colours and sizes and some had to be dug out of the sand with her fingernails. She was absorbed in this task when a woman she had never seen before took her by the hand.

"Come along, child, you've strayed from your group." The woman pulled her in the opposite direction to the ice cream van.

"What about my ice cream?" Laura asked the woman.

"You can have one later, with all your friends," was the reply. Laura was confused. In her short life she had met many adults and had often been taken to places by people she did not know. But today she thought she would stay with Auntie Fid all day.

They reached some people, sitting around a big tablecloth, eating food. There were lots of children and two big, fat ladies. They were all brown.

"I found this child at the ice cream van, on her own. I thought I'd better return her to the flock." She hurried off, giving a little wave as she left.

The two ladies stared at Laura for a moment, then one of them put her arm around her.

"Where's your family, honey? Are you lost?"

"No, I was with Aunty Fid. She's getting me an ice cream."

"Well, don't you worry, we'll look after you till we find Aunty Fid."

"Why did she bring me here?" The wonderful day was suddenly going all wrong.

"She just made a mistake, honey. She thought you were with us."

The other children stared curiously at Laura.

"Come with me," the lady said. "I'll take you back to the ice cream van."

A plump brown hand grasped hers and they set off together across the beach. When they reached the van, Aunty Fid was nowhere to be seen. Laura started to cry. She stared around, looking for a familiar face. She couldn't remember where the others were sitting.

"Don't you cry, you come and eat and Auntie Fid will find you, I promise."

They set off again, back to the brown children and the picnic. The others moved up to make a place for her and the big ladies piled food onto a paper plate.

"Hey, don't fret, it's going to be alright." The soothing voice and the chocolate cake made Laura feel a bit better. The other kids showed her their collections of seaweed and pebbles and she showed them her shells. They were about to start a game of football when Laura looked up and saw Auntie Fid in the distance. She was running, her red hair flying behind her.

"Auntie Fid!" At first she didn't hear. "Auntie Fid, I'm here!"

She stopped running and turned around. Laura ran across and leapt into her arms. "Auntie Fid, a lady took me away and brought me here!"

"Why did she do that? Haven't I told you not to speak to strangers?"

"I didn't speak to her! She spoke to me! I never said anything!"

The kind brown lady came to the rescue. She took Auntie Fid's arm. "It's alright, the woman meant no harm. She saw a coloured child and thought she belonged with us."

"Why couldn't she mind her own business? She scared the hell out of me." Auntie Fid sounded angry, but she also sounded as if she was going to cry. Laura wanted to mention the ice cream but thought better of it. She wasn't sure if Auntie Fid was cross with her.

"Bye, honey," the kind lady called after them.

"Thank you for looking out for her," Auntie Fid smiled back as she walked off, but it wasn't a real smile. It was too sad.

They walked back together to where Gran Bridie and Uncle Sean were sitting. On the way, Laura spotted the lady who took her away. "Auntie Fid, she's there! That's the lady!"

Auntie Fid hurried over to the lady. "What do you think you were doing, taking my little girl off like that?" Auntie Fid was almost shouting. "Who do you think you are?" she said, even more loudly.

"Well, I saw that group of people and − er − naturally I thought − er − how could I have known she was with you?"

"Sure, you could have asked the child. She's got a tongue in her head."

"It's a mistake anyone could make," replied the

woman, and quickly walked away, casting a glance at them both over her shoulder.

Laura could see that Auntie Fid's cheeks were red. She took her hand. "It's alright. They were nice people. They weren't bad people like you tell me not to speak to."

They didn't speak again until they got back to where Uncle Sean and Gran Bridie were sitting.

"You've been gone a long time," said Uncle Sean. "I was getting worried."

"Oh, Sean, I think I've messed up the chances of fostering. A strange woman went off with Laura because she saw some coloured women and children and she never asked, she just marched her off and took her to them. I was only buying an ice cream but I had my back to her. I was waiting for my change. What's the social worker going to say now? After all those classes we've had about safety?"

Laura had no idea what all this meant, but she could tell that Auntie Fid was crying, so she put her arms around her and pressed her face against hers. "I'm sorry if I did something wrong. I'll be good now, honest!"

Auntie Fid stroked Laura's hair as she often did, winding a lock round her fingers. "You've done nothing wrong, darling." Her voice was softer. "What lovely black curls!"

Laura felt safe as she heard those words. She hadn't been naughty after all. "Can I have an ice cream now?"

# CHAPTER 12

The following week, Auntie Barbara took her to see a lady called Angela. They had met before, many times, and Angela was always interested in what Laura was up to. She was smiling so Laura knew it wasn't anything bad.

"You no longer have to go the doctor's every week. They don't want to see you until September. You've done so well and done as you were told, and you're better now. And you don't need to go to the school for poorly children anymore. After the summer holidays you'll be going to an ordinary school."

Laura had no idea how another school would differ from her own. She was still trying to take this in when Angela said something even more puzzling. "You're going to live with Auntie Fid's family. They're going to take care of you. Would you like that?"

Laura wasn't sure. So many changes at once! It was hard to take it all in.

"You can come and see me from time to time to tell me how things are going," Angela said. She had a sweet, low voice that made Laura want to tell her secrets.

"I think I'd like it. Would I be able to see Auntie Barbara and the other kids sometimes?"

"Yes, of course. I'll make sure of that."

Angela could do anything. Laura knew that for certain.

Laura left the special school when it broke up for the summer. The teachers were really nice and gave her presents of books and sweets. Teachers and children all hugged her goodbye on the last day.

After tea, Auntie Barbara helped her pack and she set off for her new life. That night, alone in the tiny box room at the Flanagans', she thought about the other kids at Auntie Barbara's. Four of them shared a room there. They were always getting into trouble for talking at night. One of them breathed into something called oxygen and was supposed to rest. Laura wondered if they were talking now and being shouted at. She stared at the wall. There were fairies on it with brightly coloured wings, blues and pinks and sunny yellows. She fell asleep counting them as they stretched out towards the ceiling.

Life at Auntie Fid's was a bit different than going there every Sunday. Uncle Sean and granddad Brendan were out most of the day and Gran Bridie had lots to do at home and at the church. Auntie Fid was her only companion on weekdays, and she had stopped working as a cleaner for the whole summer. They went everywhere together. Laura was used to being passed around a bit when Auntie Barbara was busy, but this didn't happen here. They went shopping together, looked at books in the library, saw films at the cinema and even visited the swimming baths so that Laura could learn to swim. Gran did the cooking and sometimes in the evenings Uncle Sean would read to her in bed while Auntie Fid went out to do people's hair. Life was wonderful. Although she missed the other children, she had never before felt so special.

One sunny day at the end of August, they went to a park at the other end of town. It was a bus ride away, which made it more exciting. There were lots of things to do and play on and Laura met two friends. They were boys about her age, but bigger than her. They all had a great time, kicking a ball around and playing hide and seek. Auntie Fid sat on a bench with the boys' mother and kept watch.

Laura went across when the ball rolled under the bench. "I'm always a bit anxious when we're out," she heard Auntie Fid say. "I lost her once, on the beach. It could have put paid to my chances of fostering if she'd told the social worker."

"She seems a happy child," said the boys' mother. "You've done well."

"I hope so. I'm trying my best."

"She's a lovely kid." The mum's voice was comforting.

"You should be proud of yourself." She turned to the children. "Donald and Philip! Time to go! Come on, now!"

The boys looked vaguely alike, though one was sturdy and the other slim and willowy. The lady got up, and after groans of protest, the boys held her hands and turned to go.

"Nice meeting you – er..."

"Fidelma. People call me Fid."

"I'm Paula. See you in here, no doubt. Bye."

"She was nice," said Auntie Fid as they watched them disappear through the park gates. "I wonder if we'll see them again."

They were happy days. But at last, the holiday was over and the first day at the new school arrived. Auntie Fid dressed her in her new uniform, a grey skirt and a green jumper with a badge on it. All the adults in the house gathered round to take photographs.

The classroom was the same size as the one at the old school but there were many more people in it than her previous classroom. Lessons were longer but more interesting. The day went well and Laura had lots to tell the adults when she got home.

The next day, however, was a little different. She made friends with another child who was new, called Sarah and they played together at break time. All went well until a boy from her class came up and said to Sarah, "Don't play with her, she's a nigger. My dad says so."

"What does that mean?" asked Sarah.

"It means she's dirty. Keep away."

"Don't listen to him!" said Laura. How dare this boy interfere? "I had a bath this morning, before school. I'm lovely and clean, and you're a nasty boy!"

The boy made a silly face and shouted "Nigger! Nig..." He couldn't get the rest of the insult out because Laura, much the smaller and the lighter of the two, knocked him over.

"What's going on? Why did you push that boy?" The teacher on playground duty came across as the boy started crying noisily.

"He says I'm dirty, Miss. I'm not, honest!"

"I'm sure you're not. But that's no reason to strike another child. We don't tolerate fighting in this school."

"Does that mean I can't hit him?" Laura was unsure what 'tolerate' meant but she realised she'd done something wrong.

"I'm afraid I'll have to tell your mother," the teacher said reprovingly.

"My mother's dead. My Auntie Fid looks after me."

"Well, I'm sorry to hear that. But it's no reason to take it out on David. When did she die?" The teacher was beginning to feel a bit out of her depth. A bereavement could be causing this behaviour.

She was slightly confused when Laura answered, "She's always been dead. Since I was born."

"Mm. We'll see what your auntie says when she comes to pick you up from school."

The teacher walked away and Sarah held her hand out to Laura. They played together till the bell went and sat next to each other during lessons.

"Why did you push David at play time?" Auntie Fid asked when they got home from school.

"He said I was dirty and told Sarah not to play with me. I had a bath. I'm not dirty."

"Why would he say that?" Fid asked.

"His father told him I was a dirty nigger. What does it mean?"

"It's not a nice word. It's just a nasty way of saying you're a different colour of skin to him. Take no notice."

But Laura was unrepentant and was not going to be appeased. "I'll push him again if he says that."

She saw Auntie Fid look over to Uncle Sean as if she was going to say something in reply, but Uncle Sean stopped her with a shake of his head. Instead, Auntie Fid started laying the table for tea. A little later Laura heard Uncle Sean say, "At least she can stand up for herself." They were talking about her, but she didn't really

61

understand what it meant, except that she wasn't in trouble at home, even if she'd done something wrong at school.

A few days later, Angela, the social worker lady came to the house. Laura was given some toys to play with while Auntie Fid and Angela talked. At first, Laura played with the little plastic tea set she'd been given and made tea for her dolls. After a while, however, the conversation proved more interesting. She stayed quietly with her toys in case they realised she was listening.

"And how are things going with the rest of the family? It's really nice that Laura has some grandparents."

"They love her to bits. It's opened up their lives having a child in the house. But I'd like a home of my own."

"Are there any plans to move to your own place?"

"Well, Sean said we need to save up for a deposit and we're trying. I think he's quite happy here, though. It's going to be hard to shift him."

"It's much easier to buy houses at the moment, but that situation may not last. Now's the time if you're going to do it."

"Sure, it's easier than it was for Brendan. He spent years in Ireland trying to get the money together to come over here. I've got the money from my little hairdressing jobs to put away so, maybe one day."

"I'm so glad you took that opportunity. You've come a long way. I'm so pleased for you. You must have worked hard at the course, as well as looking after Laura brilliantly."

"She's come up against some racial prejudice at school. But she's more angry than upset. She seems well capable of sticking up for herself. She's not inherited that from her mother. Her mother was lovely, but she would never have done that."

"What was her father like?"

"Confident and clever. He knew much more than me and Sean."

"Those people get on, Fid. She'll be alright."

"She's a lot nicer than him."

"There you are, then. There's something of her mother in her."

Auntie Fid smiled. "She's a great loyal friend, just like her mother was to me. I can handle the school. We might have to move away anyway, if I get pregnant."

What did that mean? Laura looked up at Auntie Fid curiously. Auntie Fid noticed the look, and Laura quickly turned back to her dolls, but it was too late. The adults stopped talking to each other before Laura could hear any more. Angela got up to go.

"You're doing fine. I'll see how you're getting on in a few weeks' time. You know where I am if there are any problems."

Auntie Fid smiled and said "You're very kind, so you are."

This was quite boring, so Laura resumed her game with the new toys.

# CHAPTER 13

After that second day in class, Laura fought her own battles, despite the teachers' attempts to control the situation. The children settled down together and enjoyed learning, playing out and going on school trips. Laura was popular and had many friends, but Sarah remained her best buddy and they would fly to each other's defence if necessary. Long summer holidays were spent in the park with Auntie Fid or at the children's home, waiting for her to finish the cleaning. Sometimes she met Donald and Philip and played with them. Uncle Sean played games with her in the evenings, after he had taken Auntie Fid to do hairdressing in people's houses. She didn't cough much anymore and the noise that sounded like mice squeaking in her chest got less and less. Life was good.

The years at primary school were happy and secure. She heard nothing more about pregnancy or moving house, although she listened intently as often as possible. It was the best way to get to know anything at home. Money for school trips and new uniforms seemed to be organised by Angela, so she never felt as if she was short of anything. It didn't matter if toys weren't new. Occasionally she'd kick up a fuss about something she'd seen on television, but it was soon forgotten. Unaware of the consternation this caused the cash-strapped adults in the family, Laura soon moved on to another unattainable plaything. Most of the desired items eventually turned up at Sarah's anyway.

Schoolwork wasn't a problem either. She was among the brightest pupils in her class by the time the move to secondary school loomed on the horizon.

"I don't want to leave here," Laura told her teacher of four years. "I've got all my friends."

"Well, most of them will be going to the big school with you," her teacher reassured her. "There'll just be more new friends to meet. Big school is much better,

believe me. There's more to do and learn. You'll be alright,
I promise."

Laura wasn't convinced. It was an adventure, but it
was scary, too.

# CHAPTER 14

## *August 1988*

That summer, in the holidays before she started at the local comprehensive, Laura was out with Uncle Sean at the D.I.Y. store in town. Uncle Sean loaded the van with bits and pieces for the house while Laura messed around, picking flowers from the cracks in the wall and kicking stones.

As Uncle Sean got in the van a group of boys about thirteen or fourteen years old passed by. "Hey, nigger! Leave those flowers alone!" one of them shouted. The other boys started laughing.

"Don't you dare call me that! That's a bad word and you're ignorant!"

"And you're a nigger!" replied another of the group.

"I'm just as good as you! And I'm glad I don't look like you!" Laura was fearless, even though she was hopelessly outnumbered and several stones lighter.

"Laura!" Uncle Sean called from the van. "Pay them no mind and get in. Sure, they're not worth it."

"Shorr, he's not warth it! He's a paddy!" They all laughed at the attempt at Sean's accent. "Hey, have you got a bomb in there?"

The whole group fell about in mirth at such wit. Heaving a sigh, Uncle Sean opened the van door. His long legs swung over the side and, one massive shoulder after the other, he emerged from his vehicle. By the time he stood upright, the boys were running off down the street. The bravest one took a nanosecond to turn round and stick up a foolhardy two fingers as he streaked away. Sean turned back to the van, but Laura set off in pursuit.

"Uncle Sean, we can catch them!" she yelled excitedly. He caught hold of her and bundled her into the van.

"Didn't I say leave them be?"

"But they said you'd got a bomb. You wouldn't hurt a

fly."

It was true. Uncle Sean had trouble killing a bird after the cat had half eaten it.

"Laura, you can't fight everyone you don't agree with. They're only behaving like that because they're in a crowd. Sometimes you have to let things go."

"But I don't like them laughing at you, Uncle Sean."

"And I don't like them laughing at you either. But I've made my point. They won't try it again."

Laura wasn't satisfied, but she let it go. Uncle Sean was hard to argue with. He rarely got mad and he made everything seem reasonable and simple.

The big day arrived at last and Laura and Sarah walked into the massive school hall together, dressed in stiff new school uniforms which were much too big. The rumble of hundreds of conversations greeted them as they joined the entire district's eleven-year-olds confined in one room. The teachers were calling out names. Sarah's name was called and she was led off with a class of children. Laura tried to follow her with her eyes, but in the bobbing sea of heads, Sarah was lost. People were being summoned and going off with their new teachers. She wondered nervously if somehow, she'd been forgotten.

"Laura Briggs!" Her turn at last. She made her way along a corridor behind a tall, strict-looking lady in clickety high heels. A girl with olive skin and straight black hair fell unto step beside her.

"Hi, I'm Nighat. My parents are from Pakistan. Where are yours from?"

"I don't know. My mum died when I was born and my father's never met me. He's white and she was black, but that's all I know."

"Ace! I wish I was so interesting. My parents are dead boring."

"I'm Laura." They were entering a classroom.

"Do you want to sit by me?" asked Nighat, pointing at two desks.

"Yes, that'd be good."

They unpacked their bags.

"Look, we've got the same pencil case!" said Laura.

"Yes, my dad bought it for me."

"My Uncle Sean bought mine. He looks after me, with my Auntie Fid and Uncle Sean's mum and dad."

They chatted together about likes and dislikes, what they watched on telly, clothes and Barbie dolls. At break time, Laura found Sarah amongst the throngs of children in the playground.

"This is Nighat. She's got the same pencil case as me."

The three of them swapped experiences of their new classmates and teachers. Suddenly, Laura noticed a boy looking at her. There was something familiar about him. After a few seconds, she realised who he was. It was the boy who had called her a nigger several weeks ago. He looked away quickly. Laura stood up to confront him, but he turned and walked off without a backward glance. She was about to pursue him, but then decided not to. Perhaps it wasn't worth it.

"That's Rodney Woodrow." Nighat noticed Laura's gaze. "They call him Woody. He was at my primary school. He's an idiot."

Perhaps Uncle Sean was right. He wouldn't say anything on his own.

She also realised that her primary teacher was right, as well. Big school was much more interesting than little school. As the days and weeks went on she learned about subjects she'd never even heard of before. Nighat and Sarah were her constant companions but she had lots of other friends. She wasn't keen on homework and soon learned that Auntie Fid and Uncle Sean didn't know some of the work she was set. But Nighat's parents were really keen on their daughter's education. Laura and Sarah went round there two or three times a week to study together.

This became a habit that lasted throughout their schooldays. Many hours were spent in Nighat's bedroom, listening to the radio, playing records and talking about boys. Nighat's parents were very strict and she was not allowed out without her brother to chaperone her, so they often sneaked out via the garage door while the adults watched television. They would listen to music in the record shop, try clothes on in department stores or sit in McDonald's.

It wasn't until Laura was fifteen that she began to realise the lack of money in her foster family. Angela provided the necessities and the Flanagans gave her all the love and care in the world. But other girls had clothes that were fashionable as well as school uniform. They bought records and cosmetics and fancy shoes with their pocket money. Apart from a clock and a few pictures in her tiny room, Laura had no possessions. Her jeans and tops came from the local market which sold last year's seconds. Auntie Fid didn't wear makeup, so she couldn't even borrow a lipstick or mascara for school parties. She began to feel resentful and out of place. Besides money to spend, the other girls had breasts and curves and periods. Some even had boyfriends. Laura was small, flat-chested and she was sure she was infertile, despite Auntie Fid telling her that her periods would start soon and the monthly curse was no big deal anyway. She was still among the cleverest kids in the class, but so what? That wasn't cool anymore.

"Why can't I have pocket money like Sarah? When we go shopping with the other girls, I'm the only one who never buys anything."

"Well, I'm saving for a new house, Laura, so if it's money you're wanting just to fritter away on silly things, you can't have it." Auntie Fid had said this many times. They were sitting at the kitchen table, peeling vegetables.

"I'll be able to get a job of my own soon. I can't wait."

"Maybe at weekends, but your teachers want you to take your 'A' levels. I'm sure they'll take you part-time at Woolworths. Your mother worked there. Lots of the staff remember her."

"Well, I'd rather get a proper job. I'm sick of school."

"How can you say that? You used to love learning,"

Fid retorted.

"I've had enough of it now. I'm bored." Laura tossed away the half-peeled carrot in her hand to prove the point.

"That's a waste of a good brain. You could really make something of yourself and get a career later on. You could earn more money than me and Sean put together can ever do."

"I want some now. What good is it in a few years' time? You don't need money when you're older."

"Well, that's where you're wrong, 'cos you'll need it much more than you do now. There's more to buy than shoes and handbags. We can't all walk about looking like Princess Fergie."

"Well, I want some nice things now. By the time I'm your age I won't care!"

"Laura...!"

But she'd flounced off, slamming the kitchen door. Back in her little room, Laura started to cry, without really knowing why. She was sorry she'd shouted at Auntie Fid. Perhaps she should go down and apologise. But she felt too wretched and ashamed. School wasn't that bad. Everyone said sixth form was much nicer anyway. She'd look for a Saturday job as soon as she was sixteen. She fell asleep thinking about all the firms she could apply to. Perhaps her mother's workplace wasn't such a bad idea after all. There were people there who remembered Laurel and often spoke about her whenever Laura went into the shop.

Next morning she woke with a dull ache, low down in her belly. There was blood in her pyjama pants. Her periods were here at last. She looked at her chest in the mirror. The bee sting apologies for boobs were no bigger than they were yesterday, but at least she was an ordinary woman, after all.

# CHAPTER 15

## *Spring 1992*

Fid had watched the construction of the twelve-storey office block for at least a year. Work started on it, stopped after a few months or weeks, restarted with a different firm and so on until one day, she walked past on her way to work and there were people going in and out of the revolving doors. Windows were open and there was a tub of red tulips on the pavement outside. For so long it had been an eyesore. It was good to see it come alive at last.

But a nicer-looking environment wasn't her greatest concern. Soon, Laura would be sixteen and entering the sixth form at school. Although technically still a child, and the responsibility of the council, she could leave foster care if she wished. As long as the social worker approved and monitored her lodgings she could live where she liked. Fid was sure they would always remain in touch, but it wouldn't be the same.

They were still all crowded into Brendan's little house and Laura had managed in the little box room for most of her childhood. The baby Fid longed for never arrived. Her hairdressing job brought in a bit extra which she'd stashed away for a deposit on a house. She would love to move into somewhere of her own. Brendan and Bridie were getting on, but they could manage without Fid and Sean as long as they were nearby. But, sadly, she knew it would seem empty without Laura.

She had two part-time jobs and was on the way to the second one of the day as a stylist in a salon. "Hey, Linda, guess what?" she called to her workmate. "The skyscraper on High Street's finished. I just walked past and the scaffolding's down and there's people working there."

"Oh, didn't you know? They had a grand opening yesterday. You must have been at the children's home."

"Yes, I was. Did you see anything?"

71

"You didn't miss much, just a lot of speeches and faffing around and some schoolkid cutting the tape. Apparently, he'd been the star pupil and that was his reward."

"Some prize that was!" Fid retorted. "I hope he got something else as well."

"Anyway, you've got a two o'clock appointment, Fid. Better get changed."

Fid was heading for the staff room when Linda shouted after her. "Oh, they've got a little salon in there. They want somebody to run it. It's tiny, but it would do for a person working on their own. It's unisex, though. I meant to tell you in case you were interested."

"What hours do they want?"

"Every afternoon," said Linda. "But you don't finish till after six. It's too late for me to pick the kids up. I'm not skilled at men's hair either. But it might suit you. Here's the number."

Fid thought about it as she worked through the day. Her present post only amounted to twelve hours a week. She spent more time cleaning. There might be more money available at this place. She could keep her hours at the children's home. And it was a new venture, a chance to put her own stamp on something. As soon as she got a minute, she rang for an interview.

The foyer was bright and cheerful and smelled of plaster and fresh paint. The sun streamed through the glass doors and showed off the clean white walls. There was an air of optimism and efficiency that raised Fid's spirits. The man who interviewed her introduced himself as Ron. He was in his thirties, charming, chatty and confident. He showed her into the room which would become the salon. It was really small and poky, but at least there was a sink and plenty of plug sockets.

"You'll have to arrange your own appointments, I'm afraid. I suggest a notice board so that people can put their names down themselves. This service was an afterthought, created as a perk for the office workers in the building, something to make working here more attractive." He was almost apologetic. "A lot of people are employed here and we're hoping they'll make good use of the facility. But you will be self-employed. Are you skilled in men's hair? We envisaged a unisex salon."

"Yes, I qualified in a unisex salon, actually the first one in this area," Fid replied.

"It may take a while to get going. Most of the staff have flexitime so they can make themselves available. I'm the building manager so I'll help with the advertising. I'll make sure everyone knows about you. Security and insurance will be your own responsibility, of course, but I can recommend some reliable companies in this building."

She was beginning to lose enthusiasm by this time. It sounded too risky and complicated. Then a group of young men walked past the open salon door, heading for the lift. They were dressed in expensive, but casual clothes. As they reached the lift doors, a boy around eighteen years old ran after them.

"Mr Ryder!" he called as the lift doors opened. A man turned round. He was smartly attired, slim and short. He let the teenager in and the lift doors closed behind them. Fid had only the briefest moment to look at Mr Ryder. The hair was shorter, the clothes more conventional, but there was no mistaking it was Carl.

Ron was still talking. He followed Fid's gaze. "That's Carl Ryder and his team, of Ryder Designs and Software. They're on the sixth floor. Mr Ryder's only here for a few weeks, until the firm gets settled in, then he's off back to London to his parent company. The rest of his team could become your clients, though."

Too stunned to speak, Fid looked down at her hands and tried to compose herself. Fearing she wasn't interested, Ron babbled on about the other tenant firms, the building, the handy location of the salon. Finally, getting no response, he said, "Would you be interested? Will you think about it?"

"I'll take it, if you'll have me."

It was Ron's turn to be speechless. A matter of minutes ago, he was certain she didn't want it. Finally, he said, "There's a deposit to pay, a month's rent in advance and the usual checks on your debt record."

"I can pay the deposit and rent in a day or so." She would beg on the streets if necessary.

"The paperwork can be ready by the end of the week, if you're sure you want to take it on." She'd never been surer about anything. "Well, nice to meet you, Mrs Flanagan. My office is just across the hall, so I can deal with any queries or problems you may come across. My door is always open. Except when I'm out, of course." He laughed a little nervously and took Fid's hand. "Here's to a good working relationship." Fid managed a smile and slowly left the building, still in a state of shock.

She made for the public toilets and sat there for some time, trying to gather her thoughts. Somehow she was going to get Carl. The rent and the deposit on the tiny salon would take all her house savings. She would have to borrow equipment and go into debt to buy products. But it would be worth it because eventually she'd make Carl face up to his responsibilities. If nothing else, Laura could have some money out of him. He was obviously loaded.

# CHAPTER 16

The first stop she made was to the local library. She needed to get her facts straight. Then she called in at her place of work. The other stylists were thrilled that Fid was taking on the business.

"We'll miss you, Fid, but we wish you all the luck in the world." Her boss spoke for the rest of the staff. "Anything we can do to help..."

"There is something. I need a new hairstyle and a change of colour."

"I'll see to that!" Linda, her closest workmate offered. "You'd look great with Princess Di's latest cut. Everyone's asking for it. And a nice, burnished auburn to tone down the ginger."

"I was thinking of a mousy brown and a long fringe. Something you'd never notice in a crowd."

"Whatever for?"

"I just want to be anonymous for a while." How could she explain? She had recognised Carl instantly. She couldn't risk being noticed by him until she was ready.

Linda was baffled, but she took it on board. "I've got a grey suit at home that was given to me. You're welcome to that. You'll fade into the background with that on."

"Thanks, Linda. You get the idea."

"What in God's name have you done to your hair?" Sean's face was a study of amazement when Fid walked into the house. "Why didn't you ask me before you did this?"

"I fancied a change."

"A change? It's more like a head transplant! I don't know you. You've had the same hairstyle since we were children!"

"Sure and isn't that the best reason on earth to do something different?"

"But why now?"

Bridie and Brendan emerged from various corners of

the house to see what the commotion was about.

"Ok, I'll tell you later. It's all part of a plan. I need you men to let me practice something on you."

Brendan and Sean looked warily at one another.

"I'm not going to like this, am I?" Sean said cautiously.

"You're not to shave yourselves from now on. I'm going to do it. I need to improve my skills."

"What? You're not coming near me with a razor!" Sean said, horrified.

Brendan was too astounded to speak. But Fid wasn't listening anyway.

"Where's that pair of glasses that Laura wore for the school play?" she asked, half to herself. She began opening drawers and cupboards. "Where is Laura, anyway?"

"Gone to Sarah's. What's this all about?" Sean was totally confused.

"I'll tell you later. Right now I'm busy." She rushed off to try on the clothes and check out the new look.

"I don't like this at all," said Sean as they lay in bed that night. "It's a daft idea and a waste of money. It might never take off as a business. You know nothing about that side of things. You wouldn't dream of doing it if Carl wasn't there."

"That's true, but I'll get him, I know. I've got to be careful he doesn't recognise me too soon. I don't want him avoiding me. He's ignored his daughter all these years. It ends here."

"He might not even know she exists," Sean protested.

"How could he not know? It was in all the papers. It was on telly, for Christ's sake!"

"There were no pictures, remember. We only had the one photograph and we couldn't find it. It was in the baby case."

"Sure, he knows the address of the home, he knows her name was Laurel. Any eejit could put two and two together."

"Fid, I don't trust him. I never did."

76

"Well, Sean, I'm going to do it whether you're in or not. There's lots of stuff in the library on DNA testing. It's a new thing. You match up his cells with Laura's."

"God, how much is that going to cost?"

"I don't care. She'll be leaving us soon. It might be the last thing I can do for her."

Sean sighed resignedly. "I can't stop you doing anything, Fid." He stroked her cropped brown head. "At least your hair will grow back. Nothing else will be the same after this."

# CHAPTER 17

It was pleasant to work in the building, which was like a small village. Fid was on the ground floor, a couple of doors away from a coffee and sandwich shop. To her surprise, Fid found she was enjoying having her own little empire. At first, the staff popped in out of curiosity but soon, word got around that she was a good hairdresser and bookings came flooding in. Most people put their names down on a list of available slots by her door, but occasionally, some clients dropped in on the off chance. Ron lived up to his word and advertised the service, explained the run of the building and brought coffees in to keep her company when business was slow. Occasionally, she saw Carl leaving at the end of the day, surrounded by trendy twenty-somethings, clutching Filofaxes. Ron was quite a chatterbox and unknowingly kept her informed of Carl's whereabouts. Ron's office was across the hall and his phone often rang as soon as he'd settled down for a chat and a cuppa in the salon.

"Oh, no, that must be Carl Ryder, nit-picking again! I thought he'd be back in London by now, but apparently he's staying for another month."

Fid was careful not to react when Carl's name was mentioned. She was proud of her own discretion. She never thought she could be so devious.

Ron had visited many places and regaled Fid with stories of his travels. His wife had left him and he seemed glad of female company. At thirty-four years old, Fid had only been to England from her native Ireland, and she was fascinated. She missed his entertaining friendship when he was away looking after other properties owned by the company. Although the money wasn't exactly rolling in, she was paying the bills.

They were taking a break together one Friday afternoon.

"It's going well," Ron told her. "You're getting good

feedback from your clients."

"Yes, people seem pleased with me. I'm enjoying it. I still do my cleaning job, but I can fit them both in."

"A few of us are going to the pub after work. Do you fancy coming along?"

"No, I can't do that."

"Husband wants his tea on the table?"

"No, he won't mind. But I've got things to do." The last thing she wanted was to show up at the pub when Carl could turn up.

"Really? I always imagined your husband to be a bit possessive."

"Why do you say that?"

"Well, the way you dress, and your hair was a lovely colour when you came for interview. You were a butterfly, now you've turned into a moth. It's his idea, isn't it? He's frightened someone else might fancy you and he'll lose you."

"No, he's not like that at all."

He moved closer to her and gently turned her face towards him.

"I know you don't need these silly spectacles." He carefully removed them. "You have the most beautiful eyes. Why cover them up?"

"I..." She never finished the sentence as he kissed her softly on the lips.

"I'm sorry." He drew back. "I shouldn't have done that. Forgive me."

But Fid's lips were throbbing and a tremor began to creep through her body, making every hair on her skin stand on end. Before she could stop herself, she kissed him back, caressing his head and neck and stroking his face.

He held her close and whispered, "What are you hiding from, Fid? I won't let anything bad happen to you, I promise. You can trust me."

"Please, it's alright. There's nothing wrong at home."

"You're beautiful and gentle and resourceful. You

79

should be proud. But sometimes I think you'd like to be invisible."

"Don't worry about me."

"I'm going away to Birmingham next week, to sort out problems in one of our buildings. When I come back on Friday, I have to go to Edinburgh for the weekend. I'd love you to come with me."

"I can't do that." Fid had never been to either Birmingham, or Edinburgh. Her head was spinning and her whole body felt as if it didn't belong to her.

"Don't say no now. Think about it. You've got a whole week."

"I don't need a week. I can't do it." But the words sounded false, as if a stranger had said it. "Ron, you're going to have to go. My client's due in a few minutes." She pushed him out of the door and made a great effort to calm down. It was the last thing she had expected from herself or him. He thought she was hiding from something, not someone. He was trying to protect her. She tried to forget the kiss, but her body wouldn't let her. It had never felt like this before.

Somehow, she got through the day. And what a day it had been.

The weekend crawled by. Brendan and Bridie went out on Friday nights, so Sean rented a film to watch on Brendan's video recorder. Fid was grateful to be able to avoid conversation by pretending to be engrossed in the film. Laura chatted away about school and friends until bedtime, so her own reticence wasn't too obvious. She really didn't know what to say to Sean when he asked, "How's your day been?" – a question he asked every day. Fid was non-committal, but it was a lie, of course.

On Saturday Fid went shopping with Bridie while Brendan poked around in his shed and Sean and Laura did some gardening. She went to bed early and feigned sleep when Sean came up. In her mind she was faithful to Sean, but in her excited body and her imagination she betrayed him again and again. She tried to think of reasons, excuses why she had to go away for that weekend. She knew that whatever she told Sean, he'd believe her. He trusted her completely.

Church on Sunday offered a bit of a distraction. Father Michael, now doddery and forgetful, stumbled through his sermon while Fid day-dreamed about Edinburgh. She kept herself busy for the rest of the day. The house had never looked so clean. All the little jobs she'd been ignoring for weeks suddenly got done. By bedtime she was genuinely tired. Sean stroked her shorn head as she lay next to him. She waited guiltily for a term of endearment.

"Your red roots are showing."

Fid wanted to laugh, more at herself than Sean. Who said romance was dead?

# CHAPTER 18

Monday afternoon was quiet and dull without Ron. Fid got on with the routine chores to set up for the day's work. It was a relief to get away from the house and her own guilty feelings. She dreamed about going to Edinburgh for the weekend, even though her more sensible self was unsure if she could go through with it.

Preoccupied as she was, she didn't notice a man in the doorway behind her until he said "Any chance of a quick trim? I've got an important meeting in an hour's time."

A quick glance in the mirror confirmed it, but she knew the voice was Carl's, even after almost sixteen years. She lowered her head quickly. "Yes of course." She pointed to the chair, but Carl had already sat down.

"I'm Carl Ryder from Ryder Computer Software. I assume you've heard of me from the building manager. I see him popping in here from time to time."

Same old cocky attitude. And nosey into the bargain. He made himself comfortable while Fid's trembling hands put a cape round his neck. He was dressed in chinos, a soft, beige-leather zip-up jacket and a pair of very expensive trainers. Fid tried to compose herself. This was her moment. There might not be another. She began combing his hair at the back, keeping her head down, and wound the comb around his hair a couple of times.

"Is that something on your shoe?" she asked as casually as she could.

"Where?"

As he bent his head she pulled as hard as she could. Several hairs came out at the roots. "Oh, I'm so sorry, it got caught."

"Be more careful, for God's sake!" he said, rubbing his neck. But he was more interested in his shoes, so Fid carried on combing and snipping. They glanced in the mirror once or twice, but there was no spark of recognition in Carl's eyes.

"Do you remember a girl called Laurel Briggs?" she asked as evenly and controlled as she could manage.

"Can't say as I do." The voice was calm and light, but Fid felt the muscles in his neck contract as he spoke.

"She lived in the children's home, over in Ashwood."

"Can't say I've ever heard that name."

Fid continued talking as if he'd not said anything. "You'll be interested to know that she had a baby."

He was staring at her reflection.

"There's a child support agency now. They can make absent fathers pay for their offspring."

There was a short silence. Fid went on with the haircut.

Eventually, he answered. "You're forgetting something, Fid. The dead can't testify." The attitude was casual but the neck and shoulder muscles were rigid.

"Memory coming back, is it? You knew she died and you never came forward. I told Sean you must have found out."

"Sean! Still with the idiot gardener, then?"

"He's ten times the man you are. He's been there for your daughter all these years."

"I've got an important position, a wife in the public eye and a reputation to keep up. That child is nothing to do with me."

"You've a lot to lose if you don't pay up."

"You've got no proof, nothing. No one even knows I used to live in this town. No one who matters, anyway. I had a different name then. I don't have to answer to a former cleaner turned hairdresser."

"I'm still a cleaner, Carl. I'd rather be a cleaner than you, for all your money and fancy clothes."

"You listen to me! You cross me and I swear I'll make you sorry! That wasn't me! I'll deny it forever and I'll make your life hell! You try anything and I'll sue the arse off you!" He sprang up angrily from the chair and snatched the cape from his neck. "Here!" he pulled a twenty-pound note from his pocket. "Keep the change!

You're going to need it!"

He left with a look of fury on his face. She heard him greet somebody in the corridor, switching on the charm like a lightbulb. Fid swept the floor with shaking hands. She couldn't believe that she'd done it. All the hair was placed in an envelope and put straight into her handbag. By teatime, Carl's and Laura's samples were in the post.

Fid set off to the salon next day, head held high, dowdy suit discarded and wearing comfortable jeans and a sparkly top. The charade was over and she felt better than she had for months. Alas, the mood didn't last. As she took out her keys to unlock the salon, she saw a small notice on the door: CLOSED FOR HEALTH AND SAFETY REASONS. UNSAFE AREA.

The locks had already been changed. For a few moments she didn't know what to do next. Who did he think he was? How dare he? She wanted to confront him, show him up in his fancy office in sight of his yuppy work force. She took a lift to the sixth floor.

"Mr Ryder? He's not here. He was called to his London office this morning." The receptionist in the hallway to his suite was polite and efficient.

"Is there an address or a telephone number?"

"Are you a client?"

"Yes."

"Then you need to apply for our services through your firm. We don't deal with individuals."

Back on the ground floor, there was a lad of about eighteen at Ron's desk. He smiled politely as Fid entered the office.

"You're the hairdresser, aren't you? I've been told to give you this." He handed her an envelope and a key tabbed 'storage 64'. "We had to clear your salon for safety reasons. But don't worry, everything's in the basement."

"When will it be fit to re-open?"

"It's closed indefinitely, I'm afraid. There was a major fault in the construction."

What a load of rubbish. "I'll collect my stuff on Friday,

when Ron's back."

"Ron's staying on in Birmingham for the time being, sorting out a problem that's come up."

'So,' she thought to herself, 'Ron is being punished just for his friendship with me. He must think Ron was in on it.' She opened the envelope as she walked home. It contained a cheque returning her deposit, the three months' rent and a thousand pounds billed as 'loss of earnings'.

Sean was surprised to see her sitting at the kitchen table when he came home from work.

"You've finished early. What happened?"

"Sean, it's all gone wrong. I was half expecting Carl would get me fired but I didn't think he could move so fast. He's got it all sewn up."

"You got what you came for, Fid. Don't worry about the job. We managed before."

"I got my rent money and deposit back. He's done that so I won't be able to complain to the firm. He's got more power than I thought."

"That will replace the house money, Fid. We'll be alright." Sean's tone was comforting but the money wasn't her main concern. Fid knew that Ron was being kept out of the way because of their friendship. Carl must be worried that she'd said something. Ron was the only person she'd been friendly with. Trust Carl to notice. She'd underestimated him yet again. Sean was so nice about the whole thing that it increased her pain of losing Ron and her guilt at wanting to deceive Sean. But worse was to come. When the results came back, it was not a match.

# CHAPTER 19

Laura had dreamed that her father would one day claim her and whisk her away to a life of luxury. When she heard he was rich she'd been mentally spending his money until the test came back. Auntie Fid was sure she'd done the test wrong. Laurel never had another boyfriend. It had to be him. Laura could tell that Auntie Fid was more upset than she was. Occasionally she looked as if she'd been crying. However, dreams about absent fathers coming to the rescue were common amongst the children she met at Fid's cleaning job. None had come true so far. So, when a few weeks later, Auntie Fid started talking about investigations into Laurel's death, she was hardly listening. She watched the foster parents poring over old newspaper cuttings, night after night, and arguing over what should be done.

"It's all too late for any compensation. Anyway, she's still in care. She wouldn't get the money herself even if there was some." Uncle Sean sounded tired and defeated.

"I want to find out what happened to the other family. They might have some advice to pass on."

"Leave them be, Fid," she heard Uncle Sean answer. "You'll only upset them, raking up the past. That poor man lost his wife. It was bad enough for us. Imagine how he must have felt."

It went quiet for a while and Laura thought it was the end of the matter. School was breaking up for the summer and Laura busied herself making plans with Sarah and Nighat. Life settled down to normal again. Playing music, window shopping and talking about boys occupied her holidays. Helping Fid and Brigid with the chores and chatting on the phone passed the days and the disappointment slipped to the back of her mind.

But one evening in late August, Auntie Fid called her down from her bedroom. "Laura, I want you to come somewhere with me. Sean flatly refuses to come, and I don't feel right, going on my own. I feel I've got to meet this man. His wife died in the fire that killed your mother. But I need some support."

Laura had just settled down with her favourite Wham album, but Auntie Fid looked worried, so she said she'd go, albeit ungraciously. They set off on the bus. It was a late summer evening. They arrived at a tree-lined avenue with terraces of old, three-storey red brick houses on both sides. The last rays of the sun deepened the colours and enriched the hues of the rooftops, the sky and the leaves.

"What a lovely road!" Laura began to feel a bit less disgruntled at having been dragged along on some mystery errand. Fid didn't answer and seemed nervous and preoccupied. They rang the bell of one of the big houses and a tall, slight black man came to the door. Laura noticed he had nice eyes.

"Thanks for seeing us, Mr Moss," said Auntie Fid shyly.

"I'm Ben, please call me Ben," answered the stranger, holding out his hand. He led them up two flights of stairs to a large, airy living room. The walls were covered with paintings. There was a large one which fascinated Laura. It was almost life-size and depicted a naked, heavily pregnant woman. Her hair was long and blonde and curled down over her shoulders. She was smiling. On the frame was written 'Karen and Isobel'. There was a faded black and white photo beside it, of the same person, but much younger, dressed in a full-length old-fashioned dress and standing next to a bride. There was something vaguely familiar about her face. Maybe she'd seen one of those pictures before somewhere. She definitely reminded her of someone.

Ben and Auntie Fid were in deep conversation about boring things. Music was blaring out from another room and Ben interrupted himself to shout, "Izzie, turn that racket down!"

A girl around her own age came to the doorway, dancing to the music. She was tall and slim, with long legs.

She stopped dancing when she saw the visitors and stood, embarrassed, motionless and awkward.

Laura recognised something about her, but she wasn't sure what. Had she seen her at school? She turned back to the painting. She hadn't noticed that the adults had stopped talking. Then, suddenly she knew. A shiver went through her body from head to toe and she heard her own voice say, "It's not Karen and Isobel. It's Karen and Laura."

But no one was listening. Ben was staring at her with a strange expression on his face. She turned to Auntie Fid, but her eyes were fixed on the girl with the same expression as Ben's. They both looked as if they had seen a ghost. And indeed, they had.

# CHAPTER 20

Fid sat opposite Angela in the familiar office at the children's home. She noticed for the first time that Angela had grown older looking over the years of their relationship. Her eyes were tired and careworn and there were lines on her forehead. Had Angela seen the same changes in Fid's face?

Angela listened to Fid's sad story without comment. When at last Fid fell silent, her first words were, "I know you don't realise it, but you've committed a crime. Sending that DNA sample without permission was against the law, and pulling somebody's hair out is an assault. The man could deny it was his sample anyway. There must be hundreds of men working in that building."

The words were harsh, but Angela's manner was gentle. "I know you wanted the best for Laura."

"Oh, Angela, I did, to be sure. I was devastated to find the test came back negative. She didn't have another boyfriend. If it was somebody else it didn't bear thinking about. A carer, another child from here? It all went through my mind."

"Are you certain the other girl is his?"

"She looks just like Laurel and even dances like her. But her eyes are Carl's. I should know. I was staring into Carl's eyes for long enough."

"And what about Laura? How is she coping?"

"I wish I knew. She won't talk to me. She stays in her room all the time. When the test came back negative she took it well. She just thought I'd done it wrong, and to be honest, so did I at first. But this has really floored her. She saw a photo of the mother when she was about her age. It was on the wall at Ben's. It looked like a paler version of herself. It freaked her out. What can I do to make it better?"

"I'm afraid you can't, Fid. You've opened a can of worms. There's no way to get the lid back on. But I've every confidence in you. You can deal with it. You've been so close. She'll come to you when she's ready."

"I don't think she's told Nighat or Sarah. Normally she's never off the phone. Brendan's always moaning that people can never get through, not that anyone ever rings him anyway."

"Well, every cloud! At least you don't have to worry about the bill. Surely her friends try to ring her? They must be wondering what's happening."

"She won't see them or talk to them. I'm sick of making excuses."

"Give her time, Fid. Just be there when she's ready."

"There's something else I've not mentioned. Someone has been moved out of his job because of me. We were pals. Carl saw us chatting together, long before he recognised me, and must have thought I'd confided in him. I didn't, though. It was too dangerous to tell anyone, not even him."

There was a pause in the conversation. Angela could see the anguish on Fid's face. Eventually, she said slowly "He's quite special, then, this friend?"

Fid blushed and looked down. "It's not as bad as it sounds. Nothing happened between us."

"But you would have liked it to."

"Yes."

"And Sean?"

"I still love him, but I've never felt like this before. What have I done? I thought I was doing right. Now it's all a mess."

"I know one thing. You did it all with the best of intentions. And Laurel Briggs had the best friend in the world. It's just a pity she had such a short time to enjoy it."

"Thanks, Angela. I knew you'd understand. I don't know if anybody else will. I don't know what to do about the other family, whether to contact them or not."

"Let the dust settle. They'll be in touch."

Fid got up to leave.

"Fid?"

"What?"

"You've been a very brave person, confronting Laura's father like that."

But she didn't feel brave. She wished she'd never started the whole thing in the first place.

# CHAPTER 21

The old newspaper cuttings had been hanging around the house for ages. Laura sneaked downstairs after everyone else had gone to bed and made a few notes. It needed to be done now. She would be back at school in a week's time, facing the dreaded GCSE year. Going out without an explanation might become more difficult. Watching Auntie Fid had taught her some detective skills. A quick peek in the telephone directory gave her the contact she wanted.

She pushed Auntie Fid away when she tried to talk to her. She wasn't doing it to be awkward. She simply had nothing to say. Her whole world had crumbled into rubble at her feet. She had no idea who she was. She had more in common with complete strangers than the people she thought she belonged to. Her foster parents had never even met her mother, let alone been best friends. She didn't want to talk. She wanted to listen, to be told why she was suddenly in this hole, with no identity. She wanted to know why this had been allowed to happen.

The following afternoon, she went out, claiming she was going to Nighat's. Auntie Fid was pleased to see her up, showered and dressed and sitting down to a proper meal for once. However, lunch with the adults had been something of an ordeal which she only just managed to endure. All of them had attempted to make conversation, but it felt as if they were speaking in a different language. As she closed the front door, she heard Auntie Fid say, "Perhaps Nighat will get something out of her."

It was a relief to be away from the house. It was a hot, muggy day. Soft warm rain fell on her face and arms and evaporated on her skin. It felt good. It was the first time she'd been outside for what seemed ages.

"Hi, I'm Clara." The lady who greeted her was small and dainty. "You've no idea how wonderful it is to meet you! Come in!"

Encouraged by the warm welcome, Laura entered a small, terraced house similar to her own.

"So you're Laura Briggs. I never thought I'd meet you again. I've thought about you often and wondered if you were alright. How can I help?"

"Well, can you tell me about what happened? That's if you can remember. I've read the papers but it's not quite the same."

"I can remember as clear as day. I'll never forget as long as I live. It was the worst, and the best day of my life."

"How come?"

"Leaving your mother and the other girl behind was the most terrible thing. I was there to look after them. But they were semi-conscious. I couldn't carry them. Had I tried to drag them out we would have all died together. But I think about that, all the time. The one who got out was a bit more alert, as her anaesthetic was wearing off a little. But it was a miracle she survived the journey." Clara's eyes misted at the memory. Then she went on. "But reaching that door with you babies and that woman still alive! That was a feeling I know I'll never forget, or get again!"

"What happened after we came out?"

"I'm not sure. I fainted and woke up in the casualty department. They asked me to name the babies. Their tags had come off as it was so cramped in the cot. We still don't know which twin was born first, as they were about the same size. It was easier with you girls. You were both pink, but as I knew your mum was black, I could identify you because of your lovely, soft black hair which had the hint of a loose curl. The other baby's hair was dark brown and straight. Then they whisked you all away to whichever hospital had room for you, and I didn't even get to know how you got on. Until now."

"What about the other baby's father? Did you meet him? Did he come to visit?"

"No, the baby was transferred to a different hospital. I believe he's a really nice man. He wrote me a beautiful letter. He's an art teacher. I think they both were."

Laura had found out what she wanted to know. She couldn't tell this nice lady that she had named her wrongly. "Are you still working at the same hospital?" she asked.

Clara seemed sad when she answered, "No, I became quite ill after the fire and gave up the job. I had a lot of problems. I'm still very nervous, actually."

Laura got up. "I'd better go now. My family will be wondering where I am."

"Please stay for some tea. I'll put the kettle on."

Clara produced some warm scones and some cheese sandwiches. They chatted amiably about Laura's school, friends and ambitions. She seemed really interested, and Laura began to realise how special she must be to Clara. When she was leaving, a happy Clara came over and hugged Laura tightly. "This is so amazing! Thank you for looking me up!"

"Thank you for saving my life!" said Laura, and for the first time she realised she meant it. How lucky she was that somebody had risked her life to save her.

Back at home, Auntie Fid was waiting for her. "Where the hell have you been?"

"Nighat's."

"Well, that's a lie you've been telling me, so it is, because Nighat rang half an hour ago asking for you."

"I needed to find something out. I wanted to know why I was brought up thinking I'm Laurel's child when I'm not. I've even got her name, for God's sake! I'm nothing to do with her. I don't know who I am."

"Well, if you'd stayed in you might have found out. Ben rang asking to see you."

"Tell him no, then."

Fid gave an exasperated sigh. "See if you can do anything with her, Sean. To be sure, I haven't a clue." Fid went off into the kitchen, muttering under her breath.

"She was worried about you, that's all." Uncle Sean was almost apologetic. "We didn't know where you were, and the mood you've been in, perhaps she thought you might not come back to us. You've always had so much to say, we can't cope when you won't talk to us. We're just not used to it."

"I bet Laurel's real daughter wouldn't give so much trouble. I bet you're sorry you took me in. I'm a nobody to you."

"I'll never be sorry about that." Uncle Sean smiled as he spoke. "You see, I didn't have many friends. My parents were older when they had me and I was a bit old-fashioned. Me and Fid had always been together and I can't imagine being without her, but she nagged me sometimes to be sharper and dress more like other lads. Then you came along. You didn't care that my clothes weren't trendy or that I couldn't dance or tell stories or make witty conversation. You'd laugh at my silliest jokes. I could comfort you when you fell down. I could make you happy by reading a book at bedtime or giving you sweeties. If only it was so easy now you're older."

"But I bet you want to see this Isobel person."

"I might. Laurel loved me as I was. She never expected me to change. We were three misfits, her, me and Fid. I still miss her. I'd like to tell Isobel all about her, like I told you when you were growing up. You'll always be my little girl, though. That won't change, no matter how old you are. There's no time now for me to be as close to Isobel as I am to you. She's almost grown up. But if there was, I've got room for two."

The chatterbox was lost for words. Sean, who rarely spoke at all, had managed to reverse their roles. Fid came out of the kitchen to find Laura hugging him. Laura noticed Auntie Fid had been crying, but she was smiling now. These days she always seemed to be crying. It was nice to see a smile on her face. With a pang of guilt, Laura realised how worried Fid must have been. Perhaps she should give her some sort of explanation.

"I went to see Clara, the nurse who rescued me. I found out where she lived and phoned her."

Fid was lost for words. Bridie came in from the kitchen to listen to the conversation. "And what did you do that for, in the name of all that's holy?" Bridie's tone was disapproving.

"I wanted to know why I'm someone else's child, what happened to get me mixed up."

"And did you find out? Was it worth running off and scaring the bejasus out of us? How did we know you'd not run away after you've been behaving so strange?"

"Well, you wouldn't have let me go if I'd told you lot. Anyway, I know now. Nobody at the hospital had met Ben, so they just assumed he was white. I was the darkest baby so they thought I was Laurel's."

"I hope you didn't rant at that poor woman. She saved your life."

"I was going to, but she seemed so pleased to see me, I couldn't do it."

"Praise be to God! You've shown some sense at last! You didn't tell her about the mix-up, I take it?"

"No, I said nothing, and she's never seen Ben, so with a bit of luck, she'll never know."

Bridie gave a snort of begrudged approval, but Fid was sympathetic. "Leave the girl be, Bridie. I'm glad you're talking to us again, Laura. We've been so worried. It's such a big thing to handle on your own, but you've done it. To be sure, you're more grown up than we give you credit for."

Fid's kind words touched Laura so much that she put her arms around her and hugged her tight. "I just want to be your Laura, like I was before."

"You'll always be our Laura, so you will. No matter who else you are."

At that moment, Brendan came in from the shed. "Oh, she's out of her bedroom, then? Decided to join us again? It was so peaceful before." He winked across at Laura.

Before she could answer, Fid and Sean shouted in unison, "Shut up, Da!!"

Brendan smiled to himself and went to put the kettle on.

# CHAPTER 22

## *December 1976*

It was Christmas day. Ben drove home from the hospital along deserted roads. The journey contrasted starkly with his drive up from London two days before, when the streets were packed with shoppers, all getting into cars or on buses or hailing taxis, laden with food and presents.

It seemed so strange to him that people were carrying on celebrating Christmas when Karen was dead. How could life go on as normal? The memory of his parents' stricken faces came with him. Their devastation was almost too much to bear, especially as he could tell they were trying to be brave for his sake. His father's health was poor. How cruelly inappropriate that he should receive the phone call from the police, asking for his son, and then learn that he, with all his ailments, had outlived his feisty little daughter-in-law, so young and strong and healthy!

Ben had been the last parent to leave the special-care baby unit. Sitting by an incubator had at least given him something to do. The night staff were kind but firm. He obeyed meekly when they shooed him out. Now he found himself alone, not another creature in sight, the only person on earth.

He reached home. His flat was cold, empty and bare. Karen's presents were still wrapped and under the tree. The scent of fresh pine was something he loved and always associated with the Christmases of his childhood. Now the smell made him feel nauseous. A few days ago he and Karen hauled the tree onto the roof of his little Hillman Imp and struggled up two flights of stairs with it. Karen was only required to keep it steady, but her bump got in the way and she couldn't even do that. In the end, their neighbour Sam helped them, though he was laughing so much he could hardly lift it. That same man bumped into Ben yesterday and scurried off after a hasty greeting. Ben understood that Sam didn't know what to say to him, but the knowledge didn't decrease his sense of isolation. Normally he was happy to go unnoticed. Now, he wanted to scream, "I'm here! It's my wife that died, not me! I'm still here, more's the pity!"

He put the television on. They still had a black and white set. Karen was going to rent a colour telly for Christmas from the local shop they had always used. After a minute or so, he switched it off again, unable to concentrate, annoyed by all the inane jokes and false gaiety on all three channels. Instead, he put the radio on.

A popular song by Chicago filled the room, "If you leave me now, you'll take away the biggest part of me." After the first chorus, he could bear no more. He sat in silence, unable to find the energy to put the kettle on or look in the fridge.

There was a knock on the door. Molly, Sam's wife and Karen's best friend who lived in the flat below, called through the letterbox, "Ben, I know you're in there. Please, open the door. I've brought you something." Ben desperately wanted to sob in her arms, but part of him couldn't face her grief. He stayed motionless in his chair. Eventually she said, "I've left it on the doorstep."

When he thought she'd gone, he opened the door. There was a tray of Christmas snacks, ready to eat. As he picked it up, he noticed Molly, a few steps away down the stairs, looking up at him. Her face looked grey with sadness. They stared at each other for a minute or two. "Thanks," he managed to say. She nodded and went down the rest of the stairs. He heard her door shut as he carried the food in. Then he lay on his bed, waiting for morning when he could return to the hospital to sit with Isobel.

It was the worst day of his life so far. The funeral came close, but after his endless Christmas day, he felt he could get through the ritual of saying goodbye. Karen was not religious, so Ben wanted a small, intimate occasion. The local press was hot on the story, but he did his best not to involve them. His friends, students and work colleagues respected his privacy. Flowers were kept to a minimum and only his close friends and his parents were present at the crematorium. Ben's father, ill as he was, braved the journey. The police had managed to contact Karen's father. He was living in India as his wife's consort. Ben wrote to him with details of the ceremony, but he didn't appear. Seeing the coffin disappear through the curtains was too much for Ben and he broke down in Molly's arms. Strangely, he felt a bit better afterwards. It was the first time he'd cried in public since he'd heard the news.

Everyone who knew Karen was invited to their flat, which was safely away from prying journalists. Back in his own home, he was protected and supported. His friends and colleagues came to the wake and brought food and drinks and his mother organised the kitchen. People shared stories about Karen's strong character and big heart. Molly made a playlist of her favourite songs and became disc jockey at the record player. Ben began to relax, weeping sometimes, laughing occasionally at tales of Karen's outrageous behaviour and accepting hugs of comfort from his friends.

He noticed a stranger in the room and went across to speak to him. The man was well-built, in his late fifties and smartly dressed for the occasion. "Hi, I'm Ben. I've not met you before. Are you a friend of Karen's?"

The man was taken aback. He looked horrified, but quickly tried to conceal it. "I'm Colonel Lang, Karen's father."

"Pleased to meet you at last." Ben was polite, but he sensed the hostility in the colonel's authoritarian tone. Before they could speak further, Molly dragged Ben away to look at some photographs, apologising as she did so. When he was free again, he returned to the colonel, who was talking to the college principal and was unaware that Ben was at his side.

"I'm afraid he is my daughter's last rebellious act

against me. She's always wanted to humiliate me. She knew that in my position I couldn't entertain a mixed marriage. I can't publicly acknowledge my own grandchild. It's intolerable." Suddenly he noticed Ben. Unable to rectify the situation, he blustered on. "Er, I think you're the victim of my troubled relationship with my daughter. I'll make financial provision, of course. I..."

"Get out of my house." Ben's voice was quiet and even and all the more menacing for its control.

The man was visibly unnerved, but so sure of his authority he went on talking. "As I said, I'll take care of..."

"I won't say it again." Ben moved forward. The colonel retreated but it was too late. Ben's slight willowy frame was suddenly strong enough to seize him by the lapels of his tailored jacket and propel him out of the flat. The whole building quivered with the shock as he slammed the door in his face. The noise brought silence to the room. Someone pushed a glass of whisky into Ben's hand. He took a large gulp and felt it burn its way down.

Len, a coloured lecturer from the college, a man whom Ben had previously considered a bit of a lightweight clown, patted him on the shoulder. "Well done, mate. I'd have smashed his face in. In fact, I nearly did." Ben didn't reply, but stared at the closed door, rigid with fury. "You took on a soldier and won. These guys know what they're doing. Good on you. That bastard didn't deserve Karen. He hadn't a clue about her. You did well."

Ben still couldn't speak, so Len held out his hand. Ben clasped it in both of his. Everyone started talking again. Molly came over to hug him and Len refilled his glass. His guests stayed till bedtime and for the first time, Ben slept for four hours at a stretch.

The college gave him the whole term off. Money was tight, but he had some savings to take care of the rent and he'd sold a few paintings in London. There was a case for compensation, but he was assured by the solicitor who took it on that it would be years before money changed hands. The person who was hired to cover Karen's maternity leave was offered her job as a permanent post. She agreed to take Ben's students in her classes. She was quiet, efficient and a good artist herself, but Ben resented her. She was thirty, Ben's age, and Ben thought of her as old-fashioned and out of touch with teenage students. In fact, she was a nice woman and a perfectly good teacher. She just wasn't Karen.

The day Isobel was discharged from hospital was the scariest day he could ever remember. He'd been an avid pupil in the special-care baby unit, learned everything he could, and even stayed overnight a couple of days before she was due to come home. However, it felt so different when he was alone in the house with someone who was wholly dependent on him. He spent all day hovering over her, anxiously checking her breathing when she was asleep and cradling her all the time she was awake. Friends came and went, bringing food, doing shopping and offering endless advice. He was inundated with clothes, feeding bottles, baby equipment and offers of child minding. After that, days became so crowded he hardly had time to think about himself. Only during the nights, alone with a crying baby, did loneliness and despair descend on him like a dense fog. But somehow, he learned to live with the pain.

Gradually, life returned to some semblance of normal. Isobel went into the crèche at the college and Ben began teaching again. He and his little girl got to know each other. Every month he made the journey to London in his Hillman Imp to see his parents. The delight in their eyes made the trip worthwhile. It was also a welcome break from the sole responsibility for Isobel. After a few months, he realised he was doing what he thought he would never be capable of. Hard as it was, he was living without Karen.

# CHAPTER 23

## *1981*

The ride to Grandma's and Grandpa's was always bumpy, uncomfortable and boring. Izzie hated being stuck in a seat behind Dad, strapped in and unable to turn round if anything interesting passed by. Dad tried to amuse her with songs and nursery rhymes, and that was ok at first, but after a while his voice would tail off and she'd be singing on her own. This day was no different. Dad stopped singing and put the radio on, but it was lots of talking in big words.

"Are we nearly there yet?" she asked for the tenth time.

"Not far now," he answered, but she could tell he didn't mean it. He always used that sing-songy voice when he didn't mean it. It was going dark and some of the headlights she could see were pretty and glowed like huge, white chocolate buttons. But watching them became boring, too, so she started crying softly. Dad tried to comfort her. "It's alright, we're nearly there. Grandma will have a nice hot chocolate and a cake waiting for you when we get there."

She toned down the cries to a mumble, waiting for Dad to say something else. Nothing else was said, so she raised the volume again.

"Won't be long now," was the response. She resorted to whimpering again. Minutes passed and they still hadn't arrived, so she raised the volume. This time, Dad took no notice, so soon she was bawling her head off.

The car stopped at last. Dad lifted her out and Grandma and Grandpa met them in the lobby of their flat. Grandma hugged her and wiped her face with a tissue. "My poor baby!"

Izzie rubbed her face into Grandma's neck.

"She's been naughty," said Dad, but his voice didn't

sound cross, just tired.

"Naughty? My little Princess Isobel? I can't believe it," said Grandad, winking at Izzie. In a trice, the awful journey was forgotten. Hot chocolate and cake in Grandma's kitchen made up for everything. She loved Grandpa and Grandma's flat. It had a little balcony where she could see fields and trees. Grandma called it Clapham Common. It seemed a strange name and she could hardly ever remember it. There was a high railing round the balcony, but each leg was small enough to fit through the bars. She often sat out there, legs dangling over the edge, clasping the bar in the middle. She watched people walking dogs, jogging around the paths or playing ball. It was her favourite thing. She'd sit out there until her bottom got cold. However, it was dark when they arrived and the next morning, as she was about to thread one foot through the railings, Grandma called her in.

"We're going out today." This was unusual. They never went anywhere but the shops because Grandpa was poorly and couldn't walk very far.

"Where are we going? What about Grandpa?"

"Oh, Cindy next door is going to look in on Grandpa. Don't you worry your head about him."

Sure enough, a plump brown lady came to the door a few minutes later. "Betty, I just wanted to ask about Leroy's meals. Can you show me where you keep things? Is he on a special diet or something?"

"Lord no, he'll eat anything. I gave up trying years ago. But I'll leave his meals ready."

"As long as he's not fussy, he can eat with us," replied Cindy.

"Oh, I don't want to put you to any trouble."

Grandpa interrupted. "I'm here, you know. I'm not gaga yet. I can speak for myself. I can manage to get across the hall. I appreciate your kind offer, Cindy, and I would love to accept."

"Well, that's settled, then. In fact, you can sit and watch telly with us if you want. Joe's got the football on.

104

Come over now."

"You make sure you behave yourself, you," said Grandma. She turned to Cindy. "Mind you, I bet he'll be really charming at yours. When he's at home he never stops moaning."

Grandpa struggled to his feet and Isobel rushed to him to hug him goodbye. He smiled and winked at her as he hobbled off to Cindy's.

They took the underground to Hyde Park. When they got off the train they joined a long trail of people, all going in the same direction. It was such a big park that there was room for everyone. Grandma had made fried chicken and rice and peas, and they sat under a shady tree to eat. It was warm and sunny that day, and there was lots of space to run around and fountains and statues to look at. Dad played ball with Isobel and chased her around until he collapsed, gasping on the grass. They stayed there all day, throwing stones into the river, feeding the ducks and eating ice cream. The best was yet to come.

"Look up above!" Grandma said. Isobel looked up but couldn't see anything but clouds and a deepening blue sky.

"Don't be frightened if you hear a bang," said Dad, putting his arm round her.

Second later there was a loud noise and the sky was filled with silver, red and white stars. Isobel had never seen anything so beautiful before. All she could say was "Ooh" as more flashes and colours and patterns filled the sky. As one display faded, another was forming.

"They're fireworks," Dad explained "It's a special day."

"Nice to have a celebration all together in the park, especially after the riots," Grandma said.

Isobel had no idea what those words meant, but she guessed by the tone of Grandma's voice that celebration was good and riot was bad. She was puzzled for a second or two, but there was lots to do and see and she soon forgot. They made their way home, the same way they came, in a long queue of people heading for the underground.

Grandpa was still at Cindy's when they arrived back. "I had a great time," he told Grandma when he returned.

"What, you weren't grumbling all day and asking for endless cups of tea like you do at home?"

"I didn't need to. I was asked politely if I wanted anything. I wasn't forgotten about, like I am here."

"I had a lovely time, too, Grandpa." Isobel couldn't wait to tell him all about the fireworks, and he listened intently, nodding and smiling.

"Well, you'll be all ready to watch the wedding on telly tomorrow, won't you?"

"What wedding, Grandpa?"

"Why, it's the prince and princess, of course. I bet you'll like that. They'll all have frilly dresses and flowers and it will be in a huge church."

Isobel didn't go to church and no one she knew had got married. What was Grandpa talking about?

"When Dad put her to bed that night, she asked him about the wedding and the princess. He showed her a picture of her in a magazine. She was very pretty, but she looked like an ordinary lady, and nothing like the story-book princesses she had seen.

"Well, she doesn't go around wearing a crown on her head," Dad laughed. "And she's not a princess yet. She will be tomorrow, though."

Isobel didn't really understand, but she soon lost interest and didn't ask any more about it. But then she remembered something Grandma had said. "What's a seller something? A selly - er - celebration?"

"It means everyone having a party because something good has happened."

"So what's a riot, then? Grandma said it was nice to have a celebration, not a riot."

"People start running round breaking things because they're angry about something."

"That's really naughty. Why would people do that?"

"Well, it's usually because they feel they've been

treated badly and can't do anything else about it."

"I'd never do that."

"Oh, I hope not. I hope you never need to." Dad answered. Isobel had no idea what he meant, but she was too tired to ask any more questions and fell asleep to dream about princesses and weddings.

# CHAPTER 24

Very soon after the trip to Hyde Park, Isobel started school. She was looking forward to it. There were four others leaving the nursery to start school, but none of them lived nearby. Dad took her to meet the teachers a few days before the first day. The school was much bigger than the nursery. At nursery, she and Dad always set off together and he would come into the big room with her and laugh and joke with the ladies. Then he would walk off and disappear through a big door which she knew led to his classroom. Sometimes he took her in there when he'd forgotten something at home time. It was full of pictures on stands and smelled of paint, like Daddy's studio. She was told not to touch anything. This was hard. She wanted to mess with the strange bits and pieces she saw in there.

Everyone played together at nursery, and unless it was raining, they went outside in the garden after dinner. Sometimes she saw Dad walking around the college grounds and they would wave to each other. Isobel thought school would be like that, only bigger. But it wasn't quite the same.

The classroom was bright and cheerful with lots of interesting pictures on the walls. They weren't like the ones in Dad's classroom. There were pictures of animals and flowers and children doing things. She had seen other children wearing grey skirts and green jumpers in the other flats in the building they lived in, and she wanted to look like them. At nursery she wore trousers. She had to sit down for a long time with kids she didn't know, while the teacher asked everyone's name. At nursery she was allowed to move about as much as she liked, except at story time.

They were taken to a different room for dinner, then the parents took them home. It seemed alright. Dad took her to the park on the way home, and they fed the ducks.

They often did that when they came home from nursery together.

However, the next day, Dad said goodbye at the gate and told her that Molly would pick her up later on. After dinner she was taken back to the classroom again. There were more stories. All afternoon she looked through the window at the school gate, afraid that Molly would turn up and go away again without her. When at last the teacher said they could go, Molly was waiting at the classroom door.

"Teacher kept us for ages, after dinner," she complained. "Did she tell you that I wasn't coming home till now?"

"You'll come home at this time every day, Izzie," she replied. "That was a special day when you came home early."

This was bad news. Sitting down for a long time was boring.

"How was it? Was it fun?" asked Molly.

"You had to sit still for a long time. I don't want to go again."

"I'm afraid you have to go every day from now on." Molly's voice was kind, and Isobel trusted her. But that didn't make the information any better.

"Every day?"

"Well, except for Saturdays and Sundays. And holidays. Just like nursery."

But it wasn't like nursery. The other children didn't speak to her and she sat in a corner on her own. After a week or two, the teacher noticed that she was quiet and did as she was told.

"Isobel, come and sit here by Malcolm."

"Yes, Miss Turner," Isobel murmured and got up. Miss Turner pointed to a chair next to a boy who was always being naughty. Isobel took her place, but she hated sitting with Malcolm. Almost as soon as she sat down, he started punching her on the arm when the teacher wasn't looking. She tried sitting on the edge of her seat, to be as far away as possible, but she nearly fell off. Every so often he would whisper, "You're a blackistani, you!" into her ear.

She escaped at playtimes and dinner times, and most afternoons they could choose what they wanted to do, so Isobel always chose something different to Malcolm. But, sooner or later, they all had to return to their places.

One day, the teacher looked up and saw Malcolm hitting her. "What did you do that for, you naughty boy?"

"Do what, Miss? I didn't do anything."

"I saw you! Don't you do that again!" She turned to the blackboard and Malcolm gave Isobel another sly punch.

"He's done it again, Miss!" shouted John, a boy on her other side.

"Come out here! You can sit on your own!"

Malcolm was made to sit at the teacher's desk.

"Why didn't you tell me?" she asked Isobel. She sounded cross.

"I don't know, Miss. He's always doing it." It hadn't occurred to Isobel to tell anyone, let alone the scary Miss Turner.

A few weeks later, a new teacher came to the school. He was called Mr Ray and had twinkly blue eyes and yellow hair. He seemed much nicer than Miss Turner. He explained that he would only be with them for a o said, "You've been on this book a long time and you've got everything right. Let's see what you can do with this one."

He gave her a different one and came to see how she was getting on. "That one's too easy for you as well. Here's another." By the end of the day she had finished every workbook on the shelf. "I'm very pleased with you. You're a very clever girl."

Isobel was thrilled. No one had said that to her before, except Dad and Grandma and Grandpa.

Mr Ray left at the end of the week. All the children missed him. A few days later it was parents' evening at school. Isobel went along with Dad. She didn't understand the conversation. Miss Turner kept saying, "Well, I'm sorry that happened, but..." Isobel couldn't hear the rest.

When they were walking home, Dad said, "Why didn't you tell me that you were sitting next to a boy who was hitting you and calling you names?"

"You never asked me, Daddy," she replied. Isobel was puzzled. Dad sounded cross and he was not cross very often.

"And you were on the same book for weeks. No one monitored your progress."

She had no idea what he was talking about, but she knew something was wrong. "I'll be good, Daddy." She held tightly to his hand, almost in tears.

"It's alright, Izzie. I'm not annoyed with you." He bent down and put an arm round her shoulders. "Don't worry. School will be better from now on, I promise."

He was right. After that she didn't need to avoid Malcolm and lessons were more interesting. Miss Turner seemed to notice her more, and she was given things to do. School days became nicer. She made a friend, a boy called Teddy. His second name was Bellini, and the others all giggled when his name was called out. He was really fat. One day, she heard some older boys shouting 'Big Belly' after him. She could see he was crying so she went over and held his hand. They became friends and were friends ever after.

# CHAPTER 25

## *1983*

Eventually, Isobel made some more friends at school. The other girls all knew each other before they started, but in time, they got used to her and included her in games. Teddy remained her best friend, however, and they often met up on the park at weekends. Isobel had to wait until Dad had a free day to take her. Sometimes he had lessons to write up or meetings with students. Going to Grandma and Grandpa's was still her favourite way to spend the weekend. Once a month they would drive down on Friday evenings. The grandparents gave her everything she wanted, even though Dad disapproved. Isobel noticed that Grandpa did less and less as each month went by and he slept a lot of the time. But when he was awake, he still laughed and made jokes and called her his little princess. It was Grandma who took her shopping, let her help with the baking and knitted scarfs for her.

Then one day, when it should have been a London weekend, Dad said that they wouldn't be going until the following week.

"Oh, why? I wanted to go. Why are we waiting till next week?"

"Well, I've got a visitor coming. Someone from work."

They had many visitors. Molly and her husband Sam called in regularly and other neighbours and people from college came when Dad had a party. Dad's students often dropped by. But never had they interfered with visits to Grandma's.

"It's a really nice lady I'd like you to meet. It might be good to have another woman in the house."

But, as Isobel had never had a mother, she couldn't see why she'd want a woman around, even for a short time. "Can't she come some other time? I told Teddy we'd be going away to Grandma's, so he won't be on the park."

"Grandma knows that we're not going till next week and she doesn't mind. It's not long to wait. We'll go to the park if you want. My friend can come with us. You might find some other children to play with."

Unable to think of any more arguments, Isobel threw herself on the settee, face down. Dad didn't come over or say anything, so she took a sneaky peek in his direction. But he'd walked off into the kitchen and was peeling potatoes. There was nothing else she could think of. It was going to happen.

The next day, the lady arrived. She was called Maria, She was tall, but not as tall as Dad and she had short, dark hair which was straight and silky. She had smooth, light brown skin and sparkly eyes. She asked Isobel lots of questions, but she talked much more to Dad. They went to the park, as promised, and luckily, Teddy was there, so Isobel had someone to play with.

"Is that your new Mum, then?" Teddy asked as they sat next to each other on the swings.

"No, she's just a visitor. Why should she be my new Mum?"

"Oh, I dunno, I just thought she might be because my Mum was asking."

Isobel didn't reply, but once back at home, she began to think about Teddy's remarks. Maria went into the kitchen at teatime and helped Dad with the cooking. After tea, she showed no sign of leaving and Dad packed Isobel off to bed while Maria was still in the house. She could hear them laughing and talking as she drifted off to sleep.

She woke up a few hours later. She could hear Dad snoring, but there were other unfamiliar snores coming from the room as well. She wanted to wee, but she was too curious to go to the bathroom first. She had to see what was going on in Dad's room. There was Maria, fast asleep in the place where Isobel slept when she had a nightmare. She climbed over Dad and got into bed between them. Dad grunted and groaned but didn't wake up. Isobel snuggled up to him and fell asleep again. She was dreaming that she was in a strange house, looking for a toilet. Then she found one.

Suddenly, a scream woke her and Maria leapt out of bed and ran, naked, to the bathroom.

Dad sat up and looked round. "What's the matter?"

"She's wet the bed!" the voice from the bathroom was almost a shriek. "She's weed all over me!"

Dad looked at Isobel in amazement. "I didn't even know you were here. Why on earth didn't you go to the toilet? Change those pyjamas and go back into your own bed!"

He sounded really angry. Isobel sloped off to her own room. She left the door slightly open so that she could see what was going on through the crack. Maria was dressed again. She couldn't see Dad, but she heard him say, "I'm mortified. I've never been so embarrassed. She's never done that before. I don't usually involve her with girlfriends." Maria answered, but Isobel couldn't make out what she said. It sounded as if she was crying. "I don't get a babysitter very often, otherwise I would love to."

She said something else and jerked her thumb to the wall behind her. There was a picture of her mother with no clothes on and a big, round belly. It had been in the studio upstairs for as long as Isobel could remember, but Dad did some painting on it the week before and brought it downstairs.

"I'm sorry about that," she heard Dad say. "It was insensitive of me. I realise now that it must be very off-putting." Isobel didn't know what that meant and strained her ears to hear more but they moved into the hall. She heard the door slam and the sound of a car engine starting up.

"You're a very naughty girl. I'm ashamed of you. How could you do that? I'm really cross." He was cross all the next day. There were no treats or visits to the park, or stories. They rarely fell out, especially for such a long time. Sundays were usually their favourite day to do things together. Isobel knew she'd done something very bad.

Then on Tuesday, Dad came to school to walk her home. She usually left with another family who lived in her building and stayed with them until Dad got back from work. Dad looked really sad. "I've got something to tell you. Grandma isn't in London anymore."

"Where is she, then? Does this mean we won't be going again?"

"We'll have to go once more, but that will be the last time we go to their house."

"Why?"

"I'm afraid Grandma died. I'm so sorry."

"What do you mean?"

"Well, she's not alive anymore. Like your goldfish when it stopped moving."

This was hard to understand. Grandma had always been there for her. Surely this couldn't be right. When they got home, Molly and Sam were waiting for them. Dad invited them in.

"We're so sorry. You must be devastated." Molly took Dad's hand in both her own.

"She was always the fit one, the strong partner in her character and her health as well. My father was the creaking gate."

"It was so quick, you must still be in shock," Molly said, so quietly Isobel could only just hear her.

All this confused Isobel even more. Dad looked so sad that Isobel climbed onto his knee to hug him, forgetting that he was cross with her. He hugged her back. "I've still got you, Izzie," he said.

"Are we friends again?" she asked anxiously.

"Yes, we're friends again, Izzie."

She waited for him to tell her to be good in future, which he usually did when they fell out. But he said nothing more, just hugged her tighter than ever.

They went to London the following weekend. The journey was the same, but everything else was different. Grandad moved to another house with lots of nurses looking after him and some other old people sitting

115

around in armchairs. Dad took a few things from Grandma's flat and packed them in the car. Isobel had never heard the word funeral before, but it was mentioned lots of times by Grandma's friends. It turned out to mean a lot of singing and clapping in a big hall like the hall at school. Everyone wore hats and posh clothes. Grandpa was in a wheelchair, looking very tired.

Isobel and Dad slept in the empty flat that night. It seemed so strange to be there without Grandma and Grandpa. The next day they drove home.

"Grandpa might be able to come and live with us," Dad said as they rode along. "He just needs to get a bit stronger to be able to make the journey."

But he never did get stronger. Two weeks later they made the journey again, this time because Grandpa, lonely on his own, had gone to join Grandma.

# CHAPTER 26

## *September 1988*

Isobel was starting the comprehensive school in less than a week. Her childhood seemed to Ben to have flown by. Where had all the time gone since he brought that tiny baby home? He wished they'd done more things together. Soon, she'd be more interested in going out with friends than hanging out with her old Dad. Puberty was looming and he had no idea how to deal with it. He tried not to think about boyfriends coming on the scene. They'd been so close up until now. At the moment, she told him everything. Those days were numbered. He was relying on Isobel's shy and quiet nature to keep her out of trouble through the turbulent teenage years. Ben himself had been an obedient youngster with older, indulgent parents who gave him no cause to rebel. His worry was that Isobel would suddenly turn into Karen in a few years' time. Karen was wild, impulsive and opinionated at twenty-one when they met. He had no doubt that she'd been a handful at fifteen. But Karen had a heart of gold, and so had Isobel. Maybe that would carry her through.

He'd given up bringing a woman into the house after the disastrous incident with Maria. That relationship carried on for a few months after her brief stay at the flat, but it just wasn't strong enough to survive the humiliation on both sides. His present girlfriend was Rona, whom he met at an art fair. Rona was happy to see him at her own place, a little bachelor girl studio full of her own paintings. She came round to his flat when Isobel was at school and didn't seem to mind the picture of naked Karen on the wall. She was happy to criticise it as an art form rather than as an emotional threat.

He showed her his attic room, displayed with his own and some of Karen's paintings. She was really interested in his work. He valued her opinion and looked forward to their time together. They saw each other every Wednesday, when Isobel was at guides, and at Teddy's house afterwards. Ben would have liked more, but it suited Rona. She had her own design business, and also sold her work at craft fairs and gift shops. She was a pretty girl with long, mousy brown hair and freckles. She wore long earrings and a pendant, but apart from that, she did nothing to enhance her appearance. Except for changing her jeans and shirt, she made no effort to impress.

Ben often wondered if she noticed herself at all. Her artistic eyes seemed always to be focussed outwards rather than inwards and she spotted beauty in the ugliest of scenarios. Ben soon began to see things through her eyes. Karen had made his world much bigger. It shrank after she died, but Rona was opening it up again. She was in her late thirties but had the enthusiasm for life of a twenty-year-old. Ben couldn't imagine that diminishing, even as an old lady. She could be dreamy and impractical. Karen had taken on the world's problems. Rona didn't even notice them.

At first Ben tried to talk to her about current affairs. "Belfast's nearly as dangerous as Beirut these days," or "Ben Johnson's a disgrace. It's a bad day for sport." He would try to open a conversation. But Rona never got into a debate. What her politics were he had no idea. He missed having someone to trade opinions with. Despite this, he found he was falling in love with her.

Today was a happy day. Isobel was off on a trip with the guides. It was the last weekend before the new school year. Ben had persuaded Rona to go to the Lake District for a precious weekend away. He'd always wanted to go since moving from London. Karen travelled around as a child, in schools and with her military father; and when they met as tutors at the art college, they were both strangers to the north. They promised each other a holiday there. It was a long wait, but this was his opportunity.

Rona was thrilled with the idea. "The light is beautiful

118

up there. I can paint my new range of watercolours. I've been lots of times. It's peaceful, soothing, and therapeutic. You'll love it."

She wasn't wrong. They hired a cottage on the banks of Lake Ullswater. The trees were just beginning to turn, and tiny autumn flowers dotted the fields surrounding their temporary home. Across the vast expanse of water, the hills soared majestically, mirrored in the giant looking glass. Occasionally a ferry crossed their view, sending gentle ripples to the shore. They sat in the garden all day, painting the glorious scenery before them. In the evening, they walked to the pub in Glen Ridding and ate a meal, then strolled back to make love in their little haven. Ben couldn't remember feeling as happy for years.

All too soon it was time to return home. Rona said goodbye as Ben dropped her off at her studio.

"Come home with me for a bit. Izzie won't be home for a while yet."

"No, I must attend to my business. I'm self-employed, remember? But thank you for a wonderful weekend. And I'll see you Wednesday."

"Yes, see you Wednesday." Ben tried to keep his voice light and cheerful.

But later that day, he found himself dialling her number. "I so enjoyed our time together. I just wanted to ask if we could spend more time, and perhaps introduce you to my daughter."

"We've discussed this before. I'm happy as we are, Ben. I thought you were."

"I am. But sometimes I think I'd like to belong to a family. I took Izzie to the park last week and there were lots of other Dads. They were all going home to their wives. I had an empty house waiting for me. It would be nice to have someone to come home to."

"I can't be that someone, Ben." Her voce was soft and gentle, but the words cut him, even though she'd told him often enough before. "I don't want a child. I've never wanted one of my own, let alone someone else's, with

119

hang-ups and ideas already formed. I couldn't cope. We'd all be miserable."

"I'm not asking you to be a parent, just to spend some time with us."

"I'm sorry. I can't give you any more than we have already."

Ben wished desperately that he'd left well alone. He wanted to plead with her, declare his love, tell her he couldn't carry on without her. Instead, he said quietly, "I'll see you Wednesday. Thanks for a lovely weekend."

He knew he must respect her wishes or risk losing her altogether. He stared at Karen's picture. Alongside his painting he placed two restored photographs of her as a teenager. One showed her in jeans and a tee-shirt, being carried off by two policemen, legs in the air and arms flailing. In the other she was dressed as a bridesmaid, demure and innocent in a long frilly frock.

"Well, Karen," he addressed the painting, "Looks like I'm a one-girl guy after all."

Karen smiled down at him, sitting on her bed, naked, pregnant and happy, just as she was the last time he saw her. He traced the swollen belly with his finger. "Still got you, Izzie."

But Izzie was growing up. He resolved to make the most of now, while she was still his little girl.

# CHAPTER 27

## *August 1992*

It started off as just an ordinary day. Isobel was already in the house when Ben came in. She was making a sandwich and listening to the radio in the kitchen.

Ben called her a few times, then, getting no answer, he popped his head round the door. "Can't be bothered to speak to your old Dad, then?"

"Oh, sos, Dad. I was listening to Tony Blackburn on the radio. Teddy put a request in."

He settled down with the paper. It had been a busy day. Some woman contacted him a couple of days ago, wanting to know how he got on legally after Karen's death. He was sorry now that he'd agreed to see her. Nearly sixteen years had gone by and the financial details were hard to recall. So much had happened since then and he'd no idea where the paperwork was. But the person had lost her best friend in the fire that killed Karen. She deserved his time, if nothing else.

Both he and Isobel had come a long way since then. It was hard bringing her up, but he felt he'd done a good job. Although he wished she was less shy and reticent, she was intelligent and loyal, studious and kind and he was proud of her. She would be starting her GCSE year at the comprehensive school in a couple of weeks. There was no reason to worry about her results. Her teacher assured him she'd do alright. Teddy, her best friend, seemed to be a good influence. All his fears about her going off the rails were as yet unfounded. His life at the moment was steered into calm waters.

Isobel herself was not quite so content with life. The holidays were coming to an end and although she missed her little circle of friends, most of whom went away for the summer, she'd enjoyed the freedom from routine and the absence of homework. She and Teddy ambled round the town centre most days, listening to music in the record shops in the precinct, drinking coca cola and sharing a pick-and-mix. The next school year would be full of tests, revision, exams and lectures from Dad. People kept saying she'd do well and that they had faith in her. She wished they would leave her alone, stop putting pressure on her.

But at that moment, she wasn't anxious and didn't care what was expected of her. The music caught her up and she escaped from the dull old world and lost herself in the dance. It was a couple of minutes before she realised Dad was calling her. She yelled back, but she couldn't hear the reply, so reluctantly she turned the music down and came to the kitchen door. For the first time, she realised they had visitors. A woman and a girl around her own age were in the lounge. The girl was staring at the pictures of her mother. Dad was staring at the girl. The woman was staring at Isobel. Bewildered, Isobel looked from one face to another. Then she heard the girl say, "It's not Karen and Isobel. It's Karen and Laura."

Even more confusing. What on earth did she mean?

# CHAPTER 28

"Teddy, I just can't stand him. It's all his fault."

"How do you work that one out?"

"Well, he invited that woman round. Everything was alright before then."

"Izzie, he couldn't possibly have known." Teddy's voce was kind and tolerant. His plump body changed shape as he grew, but he still carried the hesitant manner of one who'd been bullied in his childhood. His shape didn't embarrass him anymore, but his face was now covered in spots. Isobel hardly noticed the change. He was just reliable, faithful Teddy, listening to her woes as he always did. The devastating news could only be shared with him. It was almost like talking to herself.

"How come he never noticed I didn't look like my Mum?"

"Well, he probably thought you looked like him. I know I did. Your hair's not as black and frizzy as his, but you're both long and skinny."

"Oh, thanks a bunch!" She shot a look of fury in his direction, but he didn't notice. "Now he wants to go and see that girl. I bet he's all over her. He wants me to go with him, but I'm not!"

"It might be ok, you never know."

"How could it possibly be ok?"

"I dunno." Teddy couldn't think of a reason. He was sorry he'd spoken at all. They were sitting in McDonald's, eating cheeseburgers and fries at their favourite table.

"He rang up the other day, asking to see her. She wasn't in and she never rang back."

"There you are, then. She's not interested."

"Yes, but she might change her mind."

"So might you."

"Oh, shut up, Teddy!"

"I'm only saying."

They ate on in silence, then walked home, Isobel

stamping her feet as she went, and occasionally kicking stones and litter at the wall. Teddy walked glumly at her side, sighing every now and then. At least this bad mood was an improvement. According to her father, she'd spent the last few days crying on her bed. Ben said that he was grateful that she'd spoken to Teddy and agreed to see him.

"See you tomorrow?" he said as they reached his door.

"Suppose so," Isobel mumbled back, head down and hands in pockets.

Teddy went in his house, raising his eyes to heaven. His teenage brain found it all very hard to cope with.

When Isobel reached home, Ben was cooking. "I've invited some people round for tea."

"Oh, no! I'm going out anyway. Don't think I don't know who's coming! I've had a Mackey-D's. I don't need any tea."

"Please! It might not be..." But he was talking to himself. The door slammed and she was off before he could stop her. Ben had no idea what to do. She'd been no trouble before. The news they'd had to face was tremendous and life-changing, but although they were both hurting, they couldn't help each other. Perhaps he shouldn't have invited the Flanagans round so soon. He was so curious about Laura and he suspected they would feel the same about Isobel. He was not wrong.

"I'm sorry, Izzie's gone out with her friends. She'd already made arrangements." Ben apologised as he ushered Fid, Sean and Laura into the living room. Fid and Sean's faces fell. They both smiled and sat awkwardly on the sofa, while Laura stared at the pictures of Karen on the wall. They were the only reason she'd consented to come. Ben set the table, putting an extra place in case Isobel turned up.

"What's this called? It's really nice," asked Fid when Ben served up the food.

"It's jerk chicken and tomato rice. My mother used to make it for Izzie."

"It's lovely." Sean joined in the praise.

124

Laura said nothing. She was determined not to like the house, Ben or the meal. But when Ben noticed her plate was clean, he offered some more. She found herself saying, "Yes please."

Ben tried not to show his fascination as he looked at her to serve the food.

"Your mother must be a good cook," Sean ventured, shyly.

"Oh, she was, but she passed away several years ago. They've both gone now. They were quite old when they had me."

"So were my parents. I'm lucky they're still around. I'm an only child. We live in their house. We've never managed to buy our own home."

This broke the ice. Sean and Ben had something in common. They chatted amiably about their childhoods and Fid joined in with tales of the difficulties of growing up in a big family. Only Laura, annoyed with herself for speaking at all, remained tight-lipped.

"I've got more paintings to do," Ben said as he watched Laura once more staring at the wall.

"Oh, I'm good at decorating, if you need any help. It looks very good..." Sean's voice trailed off as he realised what Ben meant by painting. He blushed scarlet and looked down at his plate in embarrassment.

"It's nice of you to offer," Ben smiled. "I might need to take you up on it sometime."

Poor Sean was unable to think of anything else to say. Ben prattled on about his childhood in an attempt to get Sean back into the conversation, but the mood was lost. He started to clear the dishes away and Fid and Sean jumped up to help, glad of a task to do.

Suddenly the door opened and Isobel burst in. The visitors all turned to look at her. She gave a furious glare around the room, then flounced off to her bedroom, slamming the door. It was Ben's turn to be embarrassed. I'm so sorry. She's taken this very badly. I don't know what to do to make it better."

125

"We understand. It must be so hard for them," Fid said.

"Laura took it very badly," Sean offered.

"Do you mind? I'm still here!" Laura retorted then immediately cursed herself for speaking yet again.

They got up to go. Ben got their coats, apologising yet again. He took a last sneaky peek at Laura as he showed them to the door. It had been a bit of a strain, but it could have been worse. They'd made a start.

Fid and Sean discussed the visit on the way home. Laura rushed on ahead.

Sean waited for a verbal battering from Fid about the painting remark. Instead, she held his hand. "I couldn't take my eyes off Isobel. I know it's hard on both of them, but I wish we'd had a conversation, just to tell her we're not going to take her from her Dad," said Fid with a regretful sigh. "Perhaps she'll come round in the end, you never know."

This was unlike Fid. There was not a word about Sean's embarrassing comment. "You didn't do too badly in there," she reassured Sean. "He seems a nice enough man, to be sure. Next time, we'll ask to see his other pictures."

"Next time?"

"We'll have go again, so we will. We owe it to Laura, even if she doesn't realise it yet. And to Isobel as well."

So that's why Fid hadn't told him off. She was too busy planning the next visit.

# CHAPTER 29

Things weren't going well for Fid. Laura wouldn't speak to Ben, Isobel wouldn't even look at Sean or herself, and neither girl would acknowledge the existence of the other. And it was all Fid's fault for prying in the first place. The atmosphere in the house was tense at the best of times and erupted into squabbles at the worst of times. Only Brendan and Bridie, both spry and alert for their age, carried on as normal, chipping in with unwanted advice at every opportunity.

Fid missed the little salon much more than she'd imagined. It was never intended to be permanent, and she still had her cleaning job, but somehow this wasn't enough. She missed her clients and the other workers in the building. But most of all, she missed Ron.

She felt disloyal admitting her feelings to herself. But she relived the memory of their kiss over and over again and part of her longed for that feeling again. She missed his friendship, too. The trip to Edinburgh, a place he'd often described, was a fairy tale, an impossible dream dangled somewhere above her head, out of reach.

So when the opportunity came to attend a health and beauty exhibition in Birmingham, she jumped at the chance. It was a weekend's work, and there was a competition for the best hairstyle. The pay wasn't much, but travel and hotel expenses were paid for. The owner of the salon she used to work for offered her the job. Fid's old position had been filled as soon as she left for Carl's building.

"It's a long two days, mind," she told Fid. "I should know, I've done it myself. The doors open at ten a.m. and don't close again till nine. You have to do anyone's hair who asks you in front of hordes of people. It's a bit like being an animal in a zoo."

"I'll risk it. I could do with the money," Fid answered.

"On the plus side, there's other things going on. It's a

huge exhibition. If you get a break, it's quite fun to look around."

Fid was happy to get away whatever, especially to Birmingham where Ron was working. It was a long shot, but she just might see him. She'd never had a weekend away before. Sean said he'd get on with some jobs while she was away and Laura was spending the weekend at Nighat's.

The exhibition hall was massive. She arrived as everyone was setting up stalls to show their wares. There were make-up stands, nail bars, pedicures, massage parlours, wig shops, tanning booths, slimming machines and of course, several hairdressers' corners. Her patch boasted four chairs, two sinks and several hair dryers of various shapes and sizes.

As soon as the doors opened to the public, Fid was busy all day. She forgot about Ron until a man in a smart suit and carrying a clip board rushed by, looking anxious. "Ron!" she called to his disappearing back. He didn't stop, but looked round. He recognised her and waved, delight on his face. Fid's heart leapt out of her body. He was here! It was more than she'd hoped for. He knew where to find her. He could come over to talk to her. She didn't dare hope for more.

But she didn't see him again that day. After a meal with the other stylists, she returned, exhausted and disappointed, to her room. She had never stayed in a hotel before. Apart from her honeymoon and trips to Ireland, she'd never stayed away from home. The luxury of her en-suite bathroom, large, soft bed and television comforted her a little. There was even a tray to make drinks and a packet of biscuits. And there was always a chance she might see him tomorrow.

The next day was even busier than the first, and Fid soon lost count of the number of coiffeurs she created.

"The last day's always the worst, especially when we've got to clear up afterwards," one of the other stylists said sympathetically.

At last, the doors finally closed on the visitors and they started packing their wares. The people who owned the cafés came round with leftover food on trolleys for the others to help themselves. Fid lingered as long as possible just in case Ron turned up. She sat among the boxes eating two pork pies and drinking lemonade, spinning them out till the other girls set off for the hotel. When the porters came to remove the goods, she gave up. Any minute, they'd be locking the doors.

"Busy day, love?" one man shouted across, seeing her sitting alone. "All over till next year, eh?" Fid smiled back. For her, it was simply all over.

Back in her lovely room, she got in the bath, using all the complimentary little jars of toiletries. After smothering herself in body lotion she put on the fluffy bathrobe and consoled herself with a cup of tea. There was a knock at the door. Cursing to herself, she got up to open it. She was in no mood to be sociable with the other stylists.

But it wasn't one of her colleagues. It was Ron. "Can I come in? I couldn't let you go without seeing you again."

"My god, I didn't think it was you. How did you know where to find me?"

He beamed at her. "I'm the building manager here, too. I knew you were coming. I saw your name on the guest list, so I chose the best room for you, Look, I've brought this." He was carrying a bottle of champagne on a tray.

"I didn't get the chance to say goodbye when you left the salon. I couldn't find your records so I couldn't get in touch. I've thought about you all the time. Here, have some champagne."

Fid had never tasted champagne before. It was sharp and fresh. The bubbles pricked her nose and tickled her throat. She felt light-headed and carefree immediately. Ron chatted about their times together while they sipped their drinks.

"I'll have to get dressed." Fid got up, but Ron took her

hand. "Please don't. You look lovely and you smell gorgeous. What's your perfume?"

"Just the free body lotion," she answered, feeling slightly awkward. She'd dreamt of this situation, but now it was here, it was very different. He leaned forward and kissed her, pushing her gently onto the bed. Despite her nervousness, she couldn't help kissing him back. He started to undo her robe, but she clutched the lapels and tried to cover herself. No one but Sean had ever seen her naked.

"I'm sorry. I didn't mean to..." he mumbled, moving away slightly.

But this was Fid's last and only chance. Despite her anxiety, she knew she must take it. Summoning all her courage, she shrugged off her robe and put her arms around him.

"Fid, are you sure this is what you want? It's ok if you don't," he whispered into her ear.

For answer, she kissed him passionately, running her fingers through his hair. She watched him undress. His skin was pale, unlike Sean's permanently weather-beaten body, and he was slim and lithe. A thin strip of black, silky hair ran down from his chest and disappeared into his pubes. Soft, smooth hands caressed her body and he smelled of aftershave and sweat. His mouth found her nipples as his hand stroked her clitoris. Though his movements were slow and calm, she could feel his heart racing against her breasts.

"Are you sure you're alright? You're trembling." His voice was full of concern.

But for Fid, there was no turning back, even if she wanted to. She had never felt like this before. Her whole body thrilled with every touch of his mouth, his tongue, his hands. "Please don't stop." This was better than the wildest fantasy she'd dared to conjure up.

He took his time, waiting until she was at ease, and when he entered her, tremors of delight coursed through her from hairline to toes, and increased with every thrust of his penis until she was almost delirious. Guilt, worries, tiredness, Sean, even the hotel all melted away and there was nothing but her and Ron's entwined bodies. Only the taste of his lips, the scent of his body and the sound of his, now heavy and excited, breathing was real.

Afterwards, they lay in each other's arms, silent and serene. Fid had never felt so relaxed before. This was a feeling worth turning her life, and other people's lives, upside down for. How could she go back to her old life after this? Ron must be part of a new life. But first she must explain about Carl and tell him what she was doing in his building. She'd hated deceiving him all that time. There wouldn't be any more secrets. She turned towards him.

"Fid," he said softly as she was about to speak. "I need to ask you not to tell anyone about this. I've wanted you ever since you walked into my office that day, looking for a job. I thought you were so lovely. I was overjoyed when you took the salon. But I'm back with my wife now. I can't risk her finding out. We can't meet again."

"What do you mean, you're back with your wife? If that's true, what are you doing with me?" Fid was taken aback. This was the last thing she was expecting.

"Well, you're married, aren't you? Don't pretend you didn't want it as much as I did." Fid had no reply to offer. "It was a stroke of luck that I saw your name in the register. I ordered the champagne as compensation for a dissatisfied customer. That's why it came with one glass. I had to use the tooth mug." He held up a plastic cup from the bathroom, grinning at his own cleverness.

He dressed hurriedly as Fid watched, stunned into silence. "You were wonderful," he said admiringly "You've no idea how attractive you are."

Suddenly aware again of her own nudity, Fid pulled the duvet over herself. Ron fumbled in his pocket and produced a plastic card. He placed it against a wall panel by the window and it slid open to reveal a fire escape leading down two floors to the ground.

"You're quite a girl, you know. Not many people could take on Carl Ryder. I wish you'd won." He gave a conspiratorial wink before disappearing through the door. The panel slid back into place. She heard the clank of his feet on the metal stairs, then silence.

Too horrified to move, Fid tried to make sense of her emotions. Disappointment and mortification battled with disbelief and astonishment. What on earth just happened? How could he? She'd felt guilty for weeks, thinking that Ron lost his job because of her. Instead, he got promoted. Whatever Carl had told him about her, Fid knew it wouldn't be the truth. None of it mattered now. She was just a stupid country bumpkin from Ireland who'd had an impossible dream. Her encounter with Ron was as brief as the brush with Carl, and just as pointless. What had she got to dream about now?

She lay in the luxurious bed, staring at the ceiling. After a while, the fatigue of the day, the sexual gratification and the champagne all conspired to send her to sleep. She woke around six o'clock, still in the same position. A long shower was an attempt to scrub away the feelings of shame and self-contempt at being so naïve. It didn't help.

She couldn't face breakfast with the others, so she crept out to the railway station and stayed there for an hour or so, until she could set off home. Once off the train, she headed straight for the children's home. It was a dry, sunny late autumn day. Brown and gold leaves were falling everywhere and there was a bite in the air. As she approached, she saw the children walking, crocodile fashion, into school. She entered the building as the carers were clearing the table and the dining room clock was striking nine. A beautiful, normal Monday morning. But how could it be? Fid's world was in pieces.

Her heart lifted a little when she saw Angela's door open and her coat on the chair.

"Whatever's the matter?" gasped Angela as a distraught Fid raced into her office and shut the door.

"Oh, I'm so glad you're here! I've been so stupid." Fid tried to go on but burst into tears.

Angela said nothing, put the kettle on and waited. Soon, after tea and biscuits, Fid managed to confide the story. "Why did he go to so much trouble, just for that one thing? And once he'd got it, he didn't even want to see me again! I don't understand."

"Are you angry?"

"Only with myself. How could I think that there was more, that I might leave Sean for him?"

"Please, don't be so hard on yourself."

"I can't help it. I feel so cheap. What can I say to Sean?"

"Do you need to tell him?" There was concern in Angela's voice, though she didn't go further or offer an opinion.

"I don't know. I'm no good at secrets, I've found that out about myself. They burn me up. But it will hurt him terribly."

"Perhaps you can protect him from that hurt, even if it makes life harder for yourself," Angela couldn't help saying. "But I know one thing you must do." She took a small packet from a drawer in her desk. "Take these morning-after pills."

"Oh, I don't need contraception, Angela. I got pregnant fifteen years ago and I miscarried. I've never used it since. I don't even have regular periods now."

"Please take them." Angela pushed the packet towards her. "One now and one in twelve hours' time. Don't complicate your life even more. If there was the faintest chance..."

"There isn't." But Fid took the pill and put the remaining one in her pocket.

"Don't forget to take the other one. You're lucky I had those. They were from the doctor for a teenager in my care. She didn't need them in the end."

"Thanks for looking out for me."

Fid was grateful for the concern, though a pregnancy

133

hadn't entered her mind. After a while, she felt well enough to tackle the cleaning and a therapeutic polishing of floors and woodwork did away with any need for conversation with her colleagues. She carried on the frantic chores after she got home and was genuinely tired when she sneaked up to bed to take her remaining tablet, tearing up the packet as she did so.

Sean came to bed sometime later and fell asleep beside her. Fid lay awake and exhausted for a long time. She'd never felt so guilty in her life.

# CHAPTER 30

Two days later, her period came, much heavier and more painful than usual. She'd been avoiding conversation with Sean by being busy and feigning exhaustion at night. She went to bed early, feeling wretched. She was curled up with a hot water bottle clutched to her stomach when Sean came to bed. He gently stroked her back and shoulders.

"I've got the curse, Sean," she said without turning round.

"I know. I just want to hold you."

She didn't speak or move. He snuggled in closer. After a few minutes' silence, he said softly, "I still love you, Fid. I always will." Still no answer. "I'll always be here for you, no matter what."

Pangs of guilt stabbed her body like sharp knives. She'd underestimated how well he knew her. Had he guessed what she'd been up to? She took the hand that was clasped round her and kissed the palm. It was large and rough and calloused. Though she loved him at that moment, she couldn't get over the disappointment of her shattered dream. Not yet.

Fid did everything she could to avoid having sex with Sean. It wasn't easy. He was desperate for the reassurance that she still cared. But, try as she might, she couldn't bring herself to make love. She feigned period pains for long after it was over, then fatigue and exhaustion were the next excuses. He stopped trying after a while. Fid knew he wouldn't complain for fear of a show-down which might end with things he didn't want to hear.

Laura was involved in school matters and seemed to be coping with the life-changing news of her identity. She became very possessive of both Fid and Sean, making conversation at every opportunity, and keeping them in sight at all times. But she was cheerful and getting on with life. However, she made no mention of Ben. Whether she discussed recent events with Nighat and Sarah, Fid had no idea. Laura refused to acknowledge the situation. If this was her way of dealing with it, then Fid felt she had to respect that. Laura was very strong. Her illness as a baby and the changes and uncertainties of her early life seemed to have given her the resilience to cope.

All the same, Fid suspected that Laura might regret passing up the opportunity to learn more about her real parents when she grew older. She decided to invite Ben and Isobel round for a meal. The hard part would be convincing the rest of her family that it was a good idea.

Brendan and Bridie were really keen. They couldn't wait to get a good look at Isobel.

"Now I'm warning you two, especially you, Brendan. Don't start asking either of them personal questions. Definitely not her, if she comes. It's all so sensitive."

"Well, I'll only be taking an interest. What's wrong with that?"

"It's nosey, you are! You can't fool me!"

"Then what am I supposed to talk about? I'll be frightened to open my mouth, so I will."

"We can only hope!"

"Bossing me about in my own house! What's it coming to?" He shuffled off to his shed, grumbling all the way.

This didn't bode well. There was a distinct lack of co-operation in the air. Bridie was more optimistic. "Take no notice. I'll keep him in check, don't worry," she told Fid, who immediately visualised an argument between Bridie and Brendan while the uncomfortable visitors looked on.

She turned her attention to Sean. "Just don't stick your size twelve boots in it, that's all I ask."

"It will be alright, Fid. They've seen us before. They know what to expect." He put an arm round her shoulders. "Stop worrying."

She looked up at him and forced a smile. He was right, of course. She was making a big deal of this. It didn't really matter what the adults said or did. Ben would come to see Laura. And Fid had no control at all on Laura's behaviour.

# CHAPTER 31

The last attempt at a get-together had gone so badly that Ben felt he couldn't ask the Flanagans round again. Perhaps he should have warned Isobel, instead of springing it on her. But he was trying to avoid a row or a disappearing act. As it was, he got both. Even so, he couldn't stop thinking about Laura. She was constantly in his mind. He had to stop himself ringing Fid for daily updates on her life and find out what school she was attending, so that he could hang out to catch a glimpse of her. But he had to play it cool. He knew he must tread carefully.

Meanwhile, he had Isobel to deal with. They'd never really fallen out before. She was hurting, and, try as he might, he couldn't help. This was the first time she'd had so big a problem and not turned to him for help, and he was devastated. He wanted to tell her that he wasn't interested in Laura, but he'd never lied to her before. He knew she'd see right through him. Her mock exams were coming up and he wanted her to do well. He needed to make her understand that he still loved her as much as before. But she withdrew from all attempts at reassurance. She would never agree to the family coming again. He toyed with the idea of a contrived meeting he could pretend was accidental but realised that was dangerous to the relationship if he was discovered.

He was saved any more indecisions by a phone call from Fid. "I wondered if you would fancy coming for a meal with us? We'd like to return the favour, so we would."

"I'd love to." This was wonderful news. "I can't speak for Isobel, of course, but I'll do my best to get her round there."

"We'll understand if she doesn't want to. But we loved her mother so much and she looks so like her. It takes me back in time. And they're around the same age. She was sixteen when I saw her last."

"Well, Isobel will be sixteen at Christmas," said Ben, and then immediately realised how silly this sounded. Of course Fid would know exactly how old Isobel was.

But Fid didn't comment. "We'll try not to stare at her. Sean and I will be very discreet. I can't rely on Sean's parents, though."

"It's alright, I'll risk it. I can take the embarrassment if Izzie storms off."

Ben was grateful for any chance of interaction.

They fixed the visit for a few days hence. Ben chose his moment to broach the subject with Isobel. One wrong word could scupper the whole thing. They were watching television together on the settee. It seemed a good time to start negotiations. Isobel loved Red Dwarf and for once, Teddy wasn't with them.

"I'm going to miss this, having someone to watch Red Dwarf with," he began. "It won't be long till you're off to university and I'll be sitting here on my own. I'll have to make the most of it." He put an arm round Isobel's shoulders and she allowed herself to be drawn towards him.

"I'll come home to see you sometimes, Dad," she answered without taking her eyes off the television.

"Yes, when you need a hot meal, or your washing doing. I went to uni. I know what it's like."

"Mm, suppose so. Shut up, anyway. I'm watching this."

He fell silent, then started again when the programme finished. "I really love you, you know, even when you're grumpy. I don't know what I'd have done, all these years, without my little girl."

But this was too much. He aroused Isobel's suspicions and she turned from the television to look at him. "You're up to something, Dad. What's brought this on?"

"Nothing, I was just..."

But she knew him too well. "I get it, and the answer's 'no'! If they're coming here again I'll be out and I won't be

139

back till they've gone!"

"They're not coming. We've been invited to theirs."

"No chance! I'm not going there to be gawped at. I bet they'd rather have that other girl than me anyway."

"I think they just want to tell you about — er..."

"Say it! My real mother! Some other woman, but not her!" She pointed to the picture on the wall.

"I'll always be your Dad. We've been through so much."

He tried to hug her, but she wriggled away and flounced off to her room, slamming the door so hard that it never shut properly again.

This was beginning to be a familiar scenario. Only a few short weeks ago he was congratulating himself on his good work in bringing her up and how calm, kind and clever she was, under his guidance. Now she was screaming at him on a daily basis. People told him it was normal behaviour at her age. So far, he hadn't confided in anyone about the abnormal circumstances they were in.

The meal was scheduled for Saturday. He had a couple of days' grace. Perhaps she would relent.

# CHAPTER 32

Isobel discussed the coming event with Teddy. "He's determined to go. I can't stop him. He wants to see that girl so desperately. He tries to hide it, but he can't wait to get round there. I bet she's a real bitch, anyway."

"Don't let him go on his own, then. You want to know what he says to her, and what she's like."

"I don't want him to like her more than me."

"He will if you keep playing him up. You need to be dead good, so that you're the favourite." To Teddy, the whole thing was quite simple.

"I think she'll be better than me at everything."

"No, she won't. You're dead clever."

"What if she's dead clever?"

"Well, she won't be better. Maybe nearly as good as you."

"I'm not going. I'll come round to yours that day. What do you fancy doing? It's on Saturday."

"I'm going away. I've got to go to Milan with my Mum and Dad. Look! I've got my new passport." Proudly, he took out an envelope addressed to Edouardo Bellini. "It came this morning. My Grandad's ill. I won't be back till after Christmas. I've got permission from school."

"Oh, great! Just when I need you here."

"You'll be ok anyway. You only want me to moan at."

"Well, so? There's nobody on my side."

"I'm on your side. But I'll be in Italy. I think you should go, just to be nosey. I'm dying to hear all about it."

Isobel realised that this was as much support as she was going to get. How like Teddy to be somewhere else when she had a crisis. Reluctantly, she admitted to herself that he had a point. This other girl might steal her Dad if she didn't watch it. Why had this happened? Why couldn't things go back to the way they were? She didn't want to admit to Teddy that she'd changed her mind. She'd tell him when he came back.

It was a lovely Saturday afternoon at the end of a mild

November, dry and with a weak sunshine and a nip in the air. Laura spotted some late chrysanthemums in the back garden. Their large, shaggy heads were a rusty bronze, contrasting with the Michaelmas daisies struggling up against the fence. She stood by the back door, a bunch of flowers in her arms. "Look, Fid! Aren't these lovely? I thought they'd be nice on the table."

"They're perfect, Laura, as we're having visitors. How did you guess?"

For a second, Laura didn't catch on. Then it clicked. "I don't want to see him. I've seen him once, that's enough."

"You mean them. He phoned to say she's coming as well."

"What did you ask them here for?"

Fid tried to explain. "Someday you might want to know where you came from. Aren't you curious? You might need him in the future. You never know."

"I've had four parents, five if you count Angela. You've all been there for me. Anyway, I can look after myself now."

"Please, Laura, give him a chance."

She didn't answer. He seemed like a nice enough bloke but she was terrified that he wouldn't like her. Why should he? And he was nothing like the father she'd dreamed about.

It was too late to rush off somewhere. Even the shed was unavailable. Grandad Brendan was in there, messing around with bits of wood and mumbling to himself. While she was still planning an escape route, there was a knock on the door. Her heart leapt into her throat as Sean led Ben into the room, followed by a girl who was almost as tall as Ben. She was slim with dark brown curly hair and olive skin.

She heard Ben say, "This is Isobel. Izzie, say Hello."

Isobel looked guardedly into Sean's face. Laura's heart gave another lurch as she saw tears in Sean's eyes.

# CHAPTER 33

It was a ridiculously awkward moment. Isobel was embarrassed by Sean's tears and looked away immediately. Laura was horrified and consumed with jealousy. Only Ben understood but even he had pangs of insecurity he tried to hide.

There was no explanation necessary, but to fill the gap, Sean said, "You look so like Laurel, so you do. It took my breath away."

He ushered them into the front room as Laura stood, silent and watching. Fid came through from the kitchen and seated them at the dining table. "It's lovely to have you here," she said, smiling. "It's like sixteen years ago and my best friend's back with me."

She saw Isobel's discomfort and could have bitten her tongue. She'd done just what she'd warned the others not to do. She busied herself with taking an ornamental candle from a cardboard box and placing it on the table. "This was given to me months ago, but we've never used it."

"It smells lovely," said Ben politely as she lit the wick, and a lavender scent pervaded the room. He placed his anorak on the chair opposite Laura's, claiming his seat where he could see her best.

Fid made conversation while Sean served the food and the talk turned to matters of the law. Should the girls seek some legal help? No one had a clue what their options were, or what, if anything, could be done to rectify the situation. Bridie came to join them at the table, bearing a homemade apple pie.

"Can't you just leave things as they are?" she asked. "What's to be gained?"

"We don't know the future, Bridie," answered Fid. "What about medical family histories, and God forbid, transplants and that?"

"Well, we need to keep in touch," said Ben. "Karen's

father is her only relative as far as I know, and he's never contacted me since the funeral, and there's no family on my side."

"Laura's social worker may be able to advise us. She's the only person I've told, so far."

"Better keep it that way," warned Ben. "At least until we're sure where we stand."

Laura was getting bored with the conversation. She tore off a piece of cardboard from the candle wrapping and began to draw flowers with the tip of the spent match. She didn't notice Ben watching her until he pulled some pastels from the pocket of his anorak and handed them to her. "Do you want to try these?"

Laura took them. They were little stubs in various colours in a small plastic bag. After a few minutes she finished the picture and tossed it aside. Ben picked it up. "Can I have this?" he asked tentatively.

"Sure, she's always doodling, the house is full of her stuff," Fid said cheerfully. "He can have it, can't he?"

Laura pushed the paper across with a nonchalant shrug but couldn't resist a furtive glance in Ben's direction.

Isobel looked on, silent and furious. She'd watched her father and his students all her life and was quite competent as an artist. But she couldn't draw like Laura. She saw Laura put the pastels back into the plastic bag.

"You can keep them," said Ben. "They're only a few odds and ends that were lying about in the classroom. I meant to throw them away." He smiled across the table at her, trying to keep his voice calm and casual.

Isobel could tell he was really impressed, but Laura had no clue, and simply said "Thanks" without looking at him.

"She's never usually so quiet," said Fid, and then immediately regretted it as Laura shot an angry glare in her direction.

"Well has everyone had enough to eat?" Fid asked, merely to dispel the awkward atmosphere.

144

"Yes, that was lovely" Ben answered. Bridie and Fid started to clear the table, refusing Ben's offer to help.

Isobel couldn't stand Ben's animated face and wandered off into the kitchen as soon as she thought no one was looking. This was far worse than she had imagined. Why on earth had she listened to Teddy? Through the kitchen window she could see a rickety shed in the small garden. Perhaps she could hide in there until it was time to go.

Sean saw her leave but said nothing until the others noticed she'd gone.

"I'm so sorry..." Ben began, but Fid interrupted.

"It's alright, we understand. Leave her be. Let her sit in the kitchen for a while."

But Isobel wasn't in the kitchen. When she opened the shed door, she found Brendan inside, tinkering with the engine of an old lawn mower. There was nothing to see but shelves of plants and boxes of tools. There was nowhere to sit except two upturned wooden boxes, one of which was occupied by Brendan. And there was definitely nowhere to hide. Startled, she turned to go.

"Oh, don't run away. It's glad I am that I've got to see you. I've been banned from the house in case I said the wrong thing and upset you. But I can see they've managed to do that all by themselves, so they have."

Isobel stood in the doorway, uncertain where to go next.

"Here, sit with me for a bit, until you feel better. I'm Sean's dad."

"Isobel." She held out a hand. Brendan took it in both his. It was cold and trembling.

"You don't need to be scared of me. I'm just a silly old man." Isobel sat down gingerly on the wooden box. "That's better. Make yourself comfortable." She did her best, among the seeding pots, nuts, bolts and other paraphernalia that Brendan collected. "Laura calls me Grandad Brendan. You can call me that if you want."

"I had a grandad. He lived in London and we used to

go to see him every month. I loved him and grandma. Except they weren't really mine, were they? They were Laura's."

"Where are they now?"

"They died, years ago. They'll never know."

"I bet they loved you back."

"Oh, they did! They really did!"

"Then it doesn't matter. You were their little girl. You must have made them happy."

Isobel smiled, remembering her trips to Clapham and how exciting they were.

"Don't mind Fid and Sean. They loved Laurel. They did everything together. Laurel was round here a lot. She liked flowers. She was shy, like you. She never said much, but if I gave her some flowers for her room, her eyes would light up, so they would. I used to bring flowers home from work, just to see that."

"Where do you work?" Isobel asked.

"Well, I don't work anymore, I'm retired, but I used to be head gardener for the council. I'd a bunch of lads working under me. Sean's one of them. He's still there."

"Do I look like her?"

"You're the image of her."

"What was my real father like?

"I only saw him a couple of times when they were out together. I never spoke to him. He was small, with blonde curly hair. Always dressed very smart, in the latest fashion. You'd probably laugh at his clothes now."

Isobel fell silent and Brendan continued messing with the engine.

After a while, Brendan said, "Do you want some flowers? There's a few left in the garden."

"I haven't got a garden at home, but I like flowers. I could put some on the table, like you do here."

"Oh, we don't usually do that. Laura picked those, but she can't be bothered, most of the time. We eat in the kitchen normally and we don't have guests very often."

The shed took up most of the back yard, but the little

borders surrounding it still had some autumn blooms. Brendan picked a bunch for her. "Do you want to go back inside, now? I'll go with you if you want."

"Yes, alright." Hopefully, it would be time to go by now.

Everyone was still at the empty table when they entered the front room.

"You ok, Izzie? We wondered where you'd gone," Ben said as he smiled up at Isobel. "I love the flowers. They'll brighten up the flat."

But Laura stood up and confronted Brendan angrily. "I wanted those flowers! I'd already picked some for the table, you shouldn't have picked anymore! You told me they'll never grow again if you over-pick them!"

This was the first time Laura had spoken at length. She shot a look of hatred at Isobel, then raced upstairs. Fid and Sean exchanged dismayed glances as Laura's footsteps thundered overhead.

"We're so sorry," said Fid.

"It's alright, I understand," Ben said, kindly. "It's very hard for both of them. It's time we were going, anyway."

"Thanks for your company. We'll do it again sometime."

"Come to us next," Ben offered, ignoring Isobel's rolling eyes. He waved goodbye as they drove off in their ancient Hillman Imp.

An hour or so after they got home, the doorbell rang. It was Sean, Fid and Laura.

"Laura's got something to say," explained Fid.

"I've come to apologise. I didn't mean it. I was such a cow."

Isobel said nothing, but Ben said, "No problem. We know it was a strange situation. Don't worry about it."

Laura could see the flowers arranged on the table. She also noticed that her drawing was pinned on the wall with a tack.

Ben watched the visitors descend the stairs to the outside door. At least he had the picture and Izzie had the flowers. And for the first time, he'd heard Laura say something more than 'yes' or 'no'. It wasn't much, but it was a tiny step forward.

No one spoke as the Flanagans' old van rattled its way home. Laura was too ashamed, and Sean felt humiliated and disappointed by Laura's behaviour. But Fid suffered the most. This situation was all her fault. She cursed the day she set eyes on Carl in the offices.

In bed that night, she snuggled up to Sean for comfort.

"How has it all gone wrong? I was only trying to help Laura and caused all this."

He didn't remind her that he'd been against the whole thing from the start. Instead, he held her tight and said soothingly, "You did a wonderful job bringing her up. It took a lot of courage to apologise. You gave her that."

Sean was always looking for the best in people. He was forever on her side. How could she have betrayed him? Guilt made her feel tender and affectionate towards him and they made love for the first time since her brief affair with Ron. It wasn't exciting, but at least she felt safe and protected. She was sorry she'd been away so long.

# CHAPTER 34

Christmas came and went. It was a strange time for both families, evoking memories buried for the rest of the year. Laura and her friends Nighat and Sarah went bowling to celebrate her sixteenth birthday and Isobel was given tickets for herself and Teddy to go to a George Michael concert. Ben promised a house party when Isobel left school in summer. He found it hard to get through her birthday, even after sixteen years.

The school holiday was boring once Christmas was over, as the days were so short. Teddy and Isobel sat around in McDonald's, making a big mac and fries last as long as possible. It was mid-afternoon and growing dark already. Teddy had just returned from Italy and prattled on about his adventures. Isobel listened enviously. Her break had been tedious and uneventful by comparison. She wasn't keen on discussing the visit to the Flanagans, but Teddy insisted on a blow-by-blow account.

"Well, even if she was a bitch, the others don't sound that bad."

"It was awful. She was awful. And Dad was all over her. And the parents stared at me all the time."

"At least she came round and apologised."

"The others probably made her come. I bet it wasn't her idea. What do you think? It wasn't, was it?"

But Teddy's attention was wandering at this stage. Two pretty girls came into the café with two boys who were swaggering around trying to look important. Teddy couldn't help gazing at the girls. He was spotted by one of the boys, who came over to their table. "What do you think you're gawping at, pock-face?" He grinned at his own cleverness.

Teddy immediately turned away and pretended he hadn't heard.

But the boy was determined to show how tough he was. "Keep your eyes for your nigger girlfriend." With a

149

smirk, he sauntered back to his companions.

"Don't call her that! She's better than you, any day!"

"Teddy, just ignore him," Isobel pleaded, but it was too late.

The boy heard and came back to their table and leered over them. "Or what, pock face? What are you gonna do?"

Teddy, trapped in his seat, backed away as far as he could.

The boy raised his fist under Teddy's nose. "Come on, or what?" said the bully, thrusting his face as near to Teddy's as he could.

"Or you'll get thrown out, that's what!" A small teenage girl was shouting at the bully's side, poking him in the ribs.

"What, by you?" he turned to Teddy and Isobel. "Is rent-a-gob going to take me on?"

"No, he is." The girl pushed a nervous assistant carrying a broom in the bully's direction.

"Ok, what're you going to do?"

The poor employee was spared having to answer as three more assistants appeared as if from nowhere and stood by his side. A man of about twenty took the lead. "I'm afraid I'll have to ask you to leave."

"Oh, and who are you to tell me what to do?"

"I'm the manager."

"Don't give me that. I don't believe you've even left school. I'm going nowhere."

"Then I'll have to call the police."

The other diners began to realise what was happening and the place went quiet. The yob turned away from Teddy to sneer at the manager, but he was outnumbered. Trying to save as much face as possible, the boy sauntered towards the door. As a last defiant gesture, he grabbed a beaker of milk shake from someone's table and flung the contents over Isobel. Then he dived through the door as quickly as he could.

For a moment, Isobel was too shocked to move. Teddy put an arm round her, but his hand was shaking.

150

The boy's companions slid out of the restaurant, trying to be inconspicuous. The staff went to get cleaning materials. Only the bossy girl seemed to know what to do. She took some paper serviettes and tried to clean Isobel's clothes.

"You really shouldn't let people get away with stuff like that. I wouldn't stand for it," she admonished them, mopping up Isobel's sodden shirt. "God, you're trembling! You've got goose pimples. He's not worth so much attention. He's just a nob-head."

Teddy was looking curiously at the girl and Isobel realised an explanation was necessary. "Teddy, this is Laura." She turned back to Laura. "Thanks for helping us. Teddy's my best friend. He knows about us, but no one else does."

"Hi, Teddy." She threw him a quick glance. "I know that guy. He used to go to my school. His acne was worse than yours. He was a prick then. He's not changed much."

The staff were hovering round, offering tissues and attempting to clean the tables.

"Come and sit with us. We're over there." Laura pointed across the room, where four teenagers were sitting together. Isobel was going to make an excuse, but Teddy gave her a warning look as he said, "Good idea. Let them tidy up round here." He led the way.

"This is Nighat, Donald, Philip and Sarah," said Laura as she pulled two chairs up.

"Hi. You two feel ok? That was rotten." Sarah's voice was sympathetic.

"I remember him from school," said Nighat. "They call him Woody. He was always picking on me, calling me Paki and telling me to put a veil on my face. Laura tried to beat him up, but I always held her back."

"I don't know why, he deserved it."

"He could make mincemeat out of you, that's why. She thinks she's wonder woman."

"I could have him, any day!"

"Oh, yeah?" said her friends in unison. Everyone laughed and Isobel felt a bit more comfortable.

151

Laura inspected Isobel's clothes. "Your shirt's a mess. I hope it's not ruined. It's ace."

"I think it'll wash out. Dad's not good at washing unless it can go in the machine. I'd rather not tell him about this, anyway. I'll have a go myself."

"If you give it to me, I'll get Fid to do it for you. I owe you one for the flowers. I was a bitch."

"Thanks, but I've nothing else to put on. My jacket doesn't fasten. The zip's gone."

"You can come home with us, we live near here," said Philip. "Our Mum's at work. We'll find an old jumper or something."

"Thanks, but..."

"We'd like that," Teddy interjected. Isobel was overruled.

They all set off together. Laura fell into step with Isobel. "Phil and Don are alright. They're twins although they don't look alike. We've been friends ever since we were small. We played together in the park near us. You don't need to be scared of them. Has Woody put you off? Cos they're not like that."

"It's alright, I've been called names before. I'm used to that. It's just — well, people I've never met. I don't know what to say to them."

"Don't worry about that. I've always got plenty to say. People tell me to shut up."

Isobel didn't answer. She wished she had Laura's confidence. No wonder Dad was so fascinated with her.

Teddy appeared to be deep in conversation with Philip and Donald. Nighat and Sarah chatted with each other, just out of earshot. Isobel's shirt stuck to her chest and she began to smell of ice cream. Laura prattled on at her side and she felt more and more awkward. Apart from 'yes' or 'no', she couldn't think of a thing to say. At last, they reached a terraced, three-storey house.

"Mum and Dad are at work," Philip assured them as he ushered them in. "Sit here while I get a jumper or something for Isobel. I'll put the kettle on."

Donald brought a monster bag of crisps from the kitchen cupboard and handed it round. Isobel began to feel less awkward and more relaxed. The boys seemed nice. Teddy was getting along fine already. He was sitting on the floor, surrounded by girls. He was intrigued by Laura, laughing at her jokes and following her conversation as she babbled on.

"Oh, God, not him as well!" thought Isobel, only just stopping herself from saying the words out loud. It was great to have him back from Italy. She didn't want to lose him to Laura.

Philip produced an old jumper and Isobel had a quick wash and changed into it.

"Fancy a video?" Donald went to a shelf by the fireplace. For the first time, Isobel noticed some birthday cards arranged on top.

"When was your birthday?" she asked.

"We were sixteen on the twenty-second."

"That's my birthday!" said Isobel.

"And mine!" Laura added. "I never knew you boys were born on the same day as me. You never..." Her voice trailed off. She stood up, staring at the twins.

"What's the matter with you?" said Sarah. She looked across at Philip. "You've managed to shut her up! How've you done that?"

"Sit down, Laura." Nighat pulled at Laura's jeans. "Let's have the video."

Laura did as she was told, and Philip put a video into the machine.

"Beetlejuice ok for everyone?"

It was.

They were sprawled on the carpet and settees, engrossed in the film, when the front door opened.

"Oh, hi, Mum!" Donald gave an apprehensive grin. "Er — just got a few friends round. We haven't made a mess, honest!"

"You better not have." She said amiably. "Anyway,

153

you'll be cleaning it up yourselves." She spotted a familiar face amongst the girls.

"It's Laura, isn't it? You used to play with the boys on the park."

"Laura and Isobel were born on the same day as us. Isn't that strange?" said Philip.

His mother looked curiously at Isobel, then turned and went into the kitchen without replying.

Teddy got up. "I think we'll be going now. Coming, Izzie? We're in the way."

The visitors all trooped out together. "See you soon. We'll be in McDonald's tomorrow," Laura said, cheerfully.

"I'll bring the jumper!" Isobel called as they shut the gate.

They all drifted off towards their homes, wondering what was for tea. Only Laura's mind was on other things. She'd recently read the newspaper cuttings about the fire, which had given her cause for thought.

Fid was preparing the evening meal when she got home. "Had a nice time?" She asked without looking up.

"I met up with Isobel and her friend. They were in McDonald's."

"Well, I hope you weren't rude to her again. Anyone can see she feels strange about the whole situation."

"No, I think we might become friends, actually. But guess what! I think I've found those twin boys who were rescued from the fire with us. Their mother saw me and Izzie and went all weird. Well, when I say found, that's silly, because they weren't lost. They've been with me all the time. It's Donald and Philip. I used to play with them on the park. I just never knew it was them."

# CHAPTER 35

## *January 1993*

It was 9.30 a.m. The bedlam generated by a husband and two teenagers getting breakfasted, washed and out of the house, had subsided. Although the room was now silent, there was an electricity in the atmosphere, quivering round the dirty dishes, discarded pyjamas and forgotten PE kits.

Paula had a whole hour to herself. This was usually her favourite time. It took a few minutes to calm down enough to put the kettle on, move aside the debris on the table and think about the girls. She was strong, she could cope, and she'd faced it all before. She took some deep breaths to steady her nerves. But try as she might, the terrible memories just wouldn't go away. The pictures in her mind floated in and out, one after another, like a slide show. The last sixteen years evaporated into a mist and she was back in the maternity ward again.

The vision of a small figure in a blue dress appearing and disappearing into a fog had haunted her dreams for months before she realised it was the woman who rescued her babies. She still had the dream occasionally, even now, but it didn't frighten her anymore.

That woman had been celebrated as a heroine and was written about on the front page of the papers for weeks. She'd even been on television. However, by the time Paula had recovered, the fuss had died down. A year later, when the midwife lost her job through ill health, there was half a column in the local rag. Paula's husband wrote an open letter of sympathy and gratitude, along with a donation to the special care baby unit. The letter was published but there had been no contact since.

She knew she would always panic whenever she smelled smoke and be afraid of touching hot metal or going in lifts, which she would always assume to be locked, but she was able to live with that. Counselling and patience helped her to live with the terrible memories which would never leave her.

But the night before the fire was a blurred memory until now. She'd watched Laura grow up with her foster mother and failed to recognise feisty little Karen in her. But the shy, frightened teenager in that ward, belittled and bossed round by an authoritative middle-aged social worker, sprang to mind as soon as she looked into Isobel's face.

Suddenly, a long-forgotten scene was filling her thoughts. They'd spent less than twenty-four hours together and, since their deaths, she'd never even seen a photograph. But she saw them now, those two pregnant girls, sitting on their beds beside her.

Paula felt she must speak to their daughters. Talking about that day would unearth feelings long buried, but she was brave enough to tackle it. She just wasn't sure how.

That problem solved itself a few days later. Laura's little gang drifted round to the twins' house and persuaded Isobel and Teddy to join them. Paula came home from work to find her living room littered with young people spread over her chairs and carpets.

"We're just going, Paula." Laura assured her, struggling to her feet.

"Well, could you hang on a minute? I'd like a word with you and Isobel." The girls exchanged worried glances. "It's alright, you've not done anything wrong. Not that I know of, anyway. Come into the kitchen."

But Paula's expression belied the reassuring speech even after she'd put the kettle on and handed out some biscuits. "I met your mums in hospital. I was the one who escaped from the fire."

Laura heaved a sigh of relief. So that was what it was all about. "I guessed that. I've read all the cuttings. Fid kept them." Paula was, for a moment, lost for words. "We got mixed up as babies and we didn't find out until a few months ago. I saw a picture of Karen and she looks like me, only blonde."

Isobel stayed silent, unsure of what to expect. This was something she hated talking about.

Paula noticed Isobel's bewildered expression. "It must be very confusing. I didn't understand why Fid fostered you, Laura. That is, until now. I remember Karen telling me she had a wonderful husband. In fact, suddenly I can recall all our conversations." Her voice trailed off and she looked really sad.

Isobel and Laura glanced apprehensively at each other, unsure of what was expected of them.

After a minute or two, Paula carried on. "Laurel was a frightened little girl with no one to tell her it was going to be alright. But she desperately wanted that baby. Karen and I promised each other that we'd stay friends and help her as much as we could. I'm afraid that we never got the chance. But at least I can tell you girls you were cherished babies. That's all I wanted to say."

So Philip and Donald were rescued at the same time as us?" Isobel asked.

"Gosh, I've known them for years and never realised," said Laura.

"Why would you? It's not something I like to talk about. I just wanted to be an ordinary mum. I didn't know why you were being fostered, Laura. It never occurred to me that you were Karen's child. How on earth did you find out about the mix up?"

"We went round to Ben's one night. That's when I saw a picture of Karen."

"Oh you poor things! What a terrible shock for you both."

"I didn't want to see pictures of Laurel. But I'm sorry now. I wish I'd seen them," Isobel said sadly.

"They've only got one photograph, but I'll get it for you." Laura's tone was kind, and Paula noticed a look of embarrassment on Isobel's face.

"Thanks. I'd like that," said Isobel without looking up.

Paula sensed an awkwardness between the two girls

and took their hands. "You two should look out for each other. It's what your mums would have wanted. There's lots to talk about."

It was Isobel who spoke first. "We'll try. In fact, Laura has already helped me, only a few days ago. A thug was calling me and Teddy names. Laura's so brave."

"I can't bear that idiot, anyway. I've been mean because I was jealous of you, Izzie. I thought Fid and Sean would like you more than me."

"How could you be jealous of me? What have I got to be jealous of? You're smart and witty and confident and I'm a wimp. Even Teddy thinks you're wonderful."

"Oh, I won't come between you and Teddy if that's what you're thinking. It'll be nice if we can all be friends."

Paula listened to this exchange with a wry smile. However painful her memories, it was worth it. She'd done something for Karen and Laurel. The fact that she'd escaped and left her two companions behind would always haunt her. But she'd helped their daughters in a small way, and she could go on befriending them. Sixteen years had passed since the brief friendship in hospital, with not even a photo to remind her. But suddenly, she saw their faces clearly, as if it were yesterday.

# CHAPTER 36

The girls met up from time to time over the next few weeks. They got into the habit of hanging out together in McDonald's or the cinema with their little gang. If all else failed, Don and Phil's house near the town centre came in handy.

Sean, Fid and Ben, though they were told about the friendship, were forbidden to interfere by inviting them round. But fate took an unexpected turn when the Flanagans had some good news.

"Guess what?" Sean came in through the back door as Bridie and Fid were at the kitchen table, having a cup of tea. "I've been offered a job. Not just any old job. It's a step up the ladder for me. Head gardener at that massive place in Manor Park."

"What, the one they're doing up?" asked Fid. She'd seen some scaffolding around a large old ruin in an overgrown field. It looked completely derelict.

"That's not all. There's a house with it. The caretaker lived in it but he's going into a sheltered flat. It needs a bit of work, but nothing I can't do myself. What do you think?" He gazed eagerly into Fid's eyes, seeking approval.

"Well, I'd have to see it, but it sounds exciting. A change might be just what we need."

"What about us?" Bridie was horrified. "You've lived here all these years. What are we going to do? Me and Brendan are too old to move. I'm seventy-five."

"You can come and see us, Mam, and we'll come and see you. We'll come every day, if you want."

"We'll look after you, Bridie," said Fid. "This is our chance. I've waited a long time for a house of my own. Not that I haven't been happy here," she added hastily.

Bridie gave a wail of discontent. "Sean's never left home. He chooses now, when we need him."

"It's fine you are at the moment, both of you," Fid answered.

"We won't always be fine."

"We'll be there for you if you're not." Fid was determined to make the most of this gift horse.

"Can I say I'll take it? I said I'd think about it. To be sure, I didn't know what you'd say. You might not like it. It's not the smart new-build you've dreamed of."

"Tell them 'yes', you eejit, before they change their minds."

"It won't ever be ours, so it won't, but the rent's really low."

"Not as low as the rent you're paying here," snorted Bridie.

"I'll have a much bigger wage, Mam. I can help you out if you need money." Sean couldn't conceal his excitement. "We can go and see it tomorrow. Come with us."

"I can't let this slip by me, Bridie. It's my own place I've been wanting all my married life. I've been saving up for years and still no nearer." After the collapse of her little enterprise, Fid hadn't managed to put anything into her house fund. Her own home became further and further away as time went by. This was something she'd never foreseen.

Eagerly, they set off the following morning. It turned out to be two cottages which had been joined together and, by the look of the conversion, this had been done several decades ago. It certainly needed a makeover, but they were both delighted with it. Even Bridie grudgingly conceded that they might do something with it.

"Wait till Laura sees it. She'll have a massive room of her own and there's a spare!" Fid was thrilled. At last they could do something nice for Laura for a short time before she went out into the world.

Laura was just as excited as Fid and Sean. She had memories of a life before she came to live with the Flanagans, but they were vague and woolly. The thought of a new house was a great adventure.

It would take a few weeks before the house was ready

to move into. Fid and Laura took all opportunities to explore the neighbourhood when they were there. It was quite a distance from the orphanage so Fid would have a longer walk to work, and Laura's school was two bus rides away. But no matter. It was well worth it.

# CHAPTER 37

Fid was thrilled to have good news to tell Angela, her social worker, who was well aware of Fid's ambition to have her own home.

"I thought Sean wasn't bothered either way, but he's just as pleased as I am. It's partly for my sake, but it's also so he can have things as he wants them. We've always had to ask Bridie about any changes we made. Now we've got a whole house to do as we like. Sometimes I can't believe it's true. He'll be great at the job, too, and it's more money."

"Does that mean you're going to give up your position here?" Angela's voice was concerned.

"No, I don't think so. I like it here. Besides, we'll never be that well-off."

"How are you getting on with Laura's real father? Ben Moss, isn't it?"

"Us adults get on fine. There's never been any bad feeling, to be sure. And the girls see each other with a group of mates. But they don't want Ben or Sean and me around. We embarrass them."

"They've made a start. It will take time. I'm asking because it occurred to me that you may hear from the absent father in the future. Carl, isn't it? And Karen's father is still alive. What if he comes looking for his granddaughter at some point?"

"I do worry about that sometimes," Fid confessed. "Especially now you can get DNA tests."

"It might be as well to get Laura's name changed to Ben's. It's a common name and it could be done by deed poll. It might put a strain on the relationships, but you've got to think of Laura. She's got no one except yourselves."

"I don't know, Angela. It seems a bit mean. What's Isobel supposed to do? We can't change her name to Carl's. We didn't even know his name until I took that job. It was probably an entirely different one when she was born."

"Give it some thought, that's all I ask. It would be my responsibility anyway. I'm still her social worker."

"Please, don't do it yet," Fid pleaded. "It's alright at the moment, so it is. I don't want to spoil it. I might be able to get the girls to accept the situation in time. They started off hating each other."

"I'll certainly warn you first, I promise."

Fid let the matter drop. But it was yet another anxiety to be pushed to the back of her mind.

However, there was the house to think about, and getting it sorted took over all other concerns. Laura pitched in with the work and dragged her school friends Nighat and Sarah along at weekends. Even the twins lent a hand, glad of a distraction from revising for GCSEs.

By early April, at the start of the Easter holidays, Sean had already cleared a patch in the grounds of the manor. A bank of golden daffodils nodded gracefully towards their cottage, just visible between the trees and rough grass. One rare, fine day, cold but with a weak sun, the Flanagans were all working at the cottage. Brendan was clearing the paths and even Bridie was happily mopping floors and wiping surfaces. Laura turned on her ghetto blaster and the song 'Friday I'm In Love' bellowed out, bringing the neglected estate to life.

Nighat, Sarah and the twins were messing around, pulling up weeds and throwing them at each other. Laura looked up to see Isobel and Teddy approaching. "What brings you here?" she asked in surprise.

"We met Donald and Philip in McDonald's yesterday and they told us what you were up to," Teddy explained. "We'd like to help if we can, that's if it's ok with you."

"Course its ok! "Laura rushed over and hugged them both in one fell swoop.

Proudly, she showed them round. There was a little outbuilding made of stone beside the cottage. Laura had already earmarked it for a den. "This will be our place. Nighat and Sarah and the twins, and you two if you want, can hang out here. It needs cleaning, but I'll make it nice."

163

Isobel and Teddy were well up for the challenge and got on with the task in hand. Soon, Isobel was enjoying herself. Laura was so full of life it was impossible not to be swept along. Then Fid and Sean received another visitor. Ben turned up, tentatively offering his services.

"I'm aware the words 'art teacher' is the definition of a wimp, but I can use a sweeping brush and a mop and fetch and carry."

"To be sure, you can do more than that. I'll be very glad to have you on board!" Sean was genuinely pleased for the help, but also for the gesture of friendship. He didn't give Ben any hard labour, but still found him useful and willing. All Ben wanted was to be near to Laura, and Sean knew that and understood.

The Easter holidays were spent painting, digging, repairing rotting window frames and washing woodwork and, although it was tiring, everyone enjoyed it. A couple of ancient sofas were in the living room and Laura claimed them for her den as soon as they were thrown out. A rickety chest of drawers, useful for resting cola bottles and crisp packets on, completed the furnishings.

The big day came at last. The old van rattled up with the back doors tied together to stop their belongings from escaping. The teenagers were there to meet them, lolling about in the den. Ben turned up with stacks of sandwiches, biscuits and fruit. Bridie brought her famous homemade potato cakes and apple pies. Fid spread out a cloth on the grass. "You lot come out of the den and help unpack!" she called sternly.

There were groans and sighs as the youngsters reluctantly emerged, changing to whoops of delight when they saw the food.

Ben hung back and found Brendan standing next to him. "This is no time for good manners. The kids will make short work of the grub, so they will. Better get stuck in." Ben smiled gratefully and did as he was told.

Laura put a tape in her portable radio cassette player and a Michael Jackson number filled the air. The young people started dancing. Without thinking, Isobel grabbed Sean and joined in. Fid looked on, tears in her eyes as she saw her best friend Laurel trying to make an eighteen-year-old Sean move to the music. So much time had passed since then, but he was just as awkward.

Laura noticed Fid's expression. "Izzie's not as shy as she used to be. She likes us now," she said as she pulled Fid into the circle.

Nighat and Donald were holding each other close. Brendan and Bridie forgot their arthritis and performed a mean jitterbug. Unloading the van could wait. This was a celebration.

# CHAPTER 38

## *May 1993*

Ben hadn't seen Rona for two years when the phone rang one evening soon after the Flanagans' move.

"Hi, I just wondered if you were doing anything tonight." Her tone was casual, as if she'd only spoken to him a couple of days before.

"Where have you been? I gave up trying to contact you years ago."

"I live in New York now. I got a contract there. I'm here for a few days, for a meeting."

Ben was speechless for a moment. He wanted to pretend he was busy, or in a relationship, or any circumstance that wouldn't class him as a loser without friends who could be picked up at the drop of a hat. But the sound of her voice made him ache to see her again.

"I can always cancel," he replied carefully. "I can come out for an hour or so."

"Great! I'd love to see you again. I'm at the Grosvenor Hotel. Can you meet me in the bar at, say, eight o'clock?"

"Yes, I can manage that."

This might prove to be a mistake, but he had to go.

Isobel was mildly curious as she watched him getting ready to go out, brushing his hair in the mirror and checking out his clothes. There was a distinct whiff of aftershave in the air as he walked past.

"You're dressed up, aren't you? I thought you were off to the pub."

"Well, I'm trying to make an effort, smarten myself up."

"Left it a bit late, haven't you, Dad?"

"What a cheek! I'm only forty-six. I'm in my prime."

"You're ancient!"

He tried to think of a retort, but 'Gladiators' came on the television and her attention strayed. Ben saw his chance and sneaked out.

Rona was just as he remembered; animated, bright, and full of enthusiasm. She was dressed in a multi-coloured skirt and a white floaty blouse. Her hair hung down to her waist and there were streaks of grey amongst the brown. She ran up to him as he entered the bar, laughing with delight.

"Well! Tell me what you've been up to! What's happened while I've been away?"

This was almost impossible for Ben to answer. "Not much, really. I'm still teaching art at the same place. Isobel leaves school this year and starts at sixth-form college in September." He really didn't feel like explaining further.

"Your life is going to get much more exciting!"

Ben gave a wry smile. Excitement wasn't what he was looking for after the last tumultuous few months. Rona prattled on, oblivious to his reticence. She was dying to tell him her news. "I've got charge of a gallery for a month. I need four artists to display their work for a week each. I thought of you straightaway."

"That sounds great, but what are the terms?" Ben's tone was cautious. Rona's ideas tended to be powered by enthusiasm and little else. She always seemed to get away with it, but Ben was never so lucky. There was bound to be a catch.

"It's free to you. I might charge the others but not you. The owner usually charges commission on all sales, and there's also a small rent fee. But someone owes me a favour, so I'm cashing in on it."

"You're using it for free?"

"That's the deal. He doesn't want to leave it empty while he's out of town. I know you could produce a collection with all that stuff in your attic."

"I'd love to do it. Where is it?"

"Well, that's the thing. It's in London."

"Hmm, it would be a bit expensive to commute."

"That's out of the question. It opens at nine and closes

167

at ten at night. Most galleries close on Mondays in London, so if you come down at the weekend you'll have time to set up. There's a studio flat above, a bit poky, but alright for one. You'll have to stay there. The caretaking is part of the deal."

Ben noticed she didn't intend to stay with him. "I'll have to make some arrangements for Isobel. Perhaps she could stay with my neighbour, Molly."

He tried to keep calm and composed, but he was overjoyed. A project like this was just what he needed to ease the turmoil of the situation with the identity of his daughter. At the very least, it was a week away at very little cost. At best, he might even sell a painting or two.

Isobel couldn't miss school at this late stage in her education, and even if she could, there was only room for one at the gallery. He'd have to convince her that staying at Molly's would be a good idea. That would probably be the hardest task in the whole plan.

"I'm in town till tomorrow night. Let me know." Rona's manner was friendly and confiding, but without any hint that romance might be on the cards. Nonetheless, Ben was thrilled to see her.

The next day he had another pleasant surprise. He came home from work to find Laura sitting on his sofa with Isobel. "Hi, Ben, I've brought this photo round to show Isobel," said Laura cheerfully, handing him a picture of four teenagers posing for the camera.

Ben's heart turned over as he looked at the old photograph. Fid and Sean were completely recognisable and the blonde, flamboyantly dressed boy who was with them was only showing his profile. But the black girl amongst them had Isobel's face, Isobel's expression and Isobel's long, slender limbs. In fact, if she were a few shades lighter, she would be Isobel.

Ben knew that he was Isobel's actual father. Her aggressive behaviour towards him since the stresses they'd endured over the past few months reassured him that she was just a normal teenager, taking her only parent's love for granted. As jealous as she had been of Laura, they both knew that he and Isobel were as close as ever. But the photograph was a poignant confirmation that, biologically, his lovely Izzie belonged to someone else.

"I've had this picture for years," confided Laura. "It was in a battered old suitcase with some baby clothes and a teddy. I wore the teddy out long ago, sorry. I loved it to bits, literally." She giggled at her own joke.

Isobel said nothing but stared at the old photo.

Ben broke the silence. "It was kind of you to bring it, Laura."

"I know how I felt when I saw that for the first time." Laura pointed to the painting and photos of Karen on the wall. "I was gobsmacked."

Isobel spoke at last. "Thanks, Laura. She looks really nice." Her voice was almost a whisper.

"Fid said she was fifteen, nearly sixteen when that was taken," Laura told her.

There was no reply, so Ben jumped in to fill the gap. "Can you stay for tea, Laura? I'm making jerk chicken and tomato rice." Ben remembered how she'd polished off the meal when she came round with Fid and Sean.

"I'm supposed to be revising."

"Well, you could do your homework together, then I'll run you home. It'll only take a few minutes now you've moved nearer to us. Perhaps we'll see more of you in future."

He stopped, annoyed with himself. Perhaps this was too much, too soon. Perhaps he had crowded her. But Laura smiled and merely said, "Yes, alright. Where's the phone? I'll tell Fid."

Despite his heartache about the picture, it was a lovely evening. Ben did his best to stay in the background, listening to the girls' conversation and observing all Laura's mannerisms and movements which were so like Karen's.

He decided to take up Rona's offer of a week in London. Isobel seemed so much calmer and more settled.

He resolved to ask Molly, his neighbour in the flat below, to take her in for the week. They had been friends for years, so, hopefully, it wouldn't be a problem.

Ben went to bed that night feeling happier than he had since the revelation that Isobel was not his daughter. He still had Isobel and was gaining a little ground with Laura, whom he found delightful. Even so, the picture of Isobel's real mother was disturbing. He'd always thought of Isobel as his child, no one else's. Perhaps he could end up with two daughters.

His decision was made regarding the London trip. Although there was no chance of a future with Rona, he knew he'd enjoy even the briefest encounter. Life was getting better.

# CHAPTER 39

## *May 1993*

Fid felt that there should be some arrangements made for Laura's future. The family received a small allowance for fostering since Laura came to live with them, but Fid was unsure what would happen when Laura left school to go to sixth-form college. Sean was earning more at this new job, so things were improving financially, but they weren't well off by any means. Fid's little nest egg had dwindled away on fittings and furniture for the cottage.

They'd been living there for a couple of weeks before she approached Angela with the problem.

"Why didn't you tell me you were worried?" Angela was mildly surprised. "I'm her social worker so it's up to me to see she's cared for. I've already been looking into it. I want it all sorted before I retire next month." She produced a file from the drawer in her desk.

"It's bothered I've been for months. In fact, since she came to me as a wee dote I've wondered what would become of her, so I have."

"Fid, since we've found out that Ben's her father, I haven't said or done anything yet, but..."

Fid's anxious expression stopped Angela mid flow. "You promised not to do anything without telling me. I need to prepare Laura!" Fid's distress was so acute that she almost burst into tears.

"I'm sorry, I didn't mean to upset you. There's a grant available so she can stay with you if she wishes, but there's also the option of her natural father adopting her. That possibility ends soon because of her age, of course."

"I don't want to lose her, and I won't stand in her way, though I'll miss her terribly, and now you're leaving us and..." Suddenly, Fid felt close to weeping. She tried to fight it off as best she could, but Angela noticed. "I'm so sorry. I've been such a softie recently, crying over nothing.

I've got a bit tired and run down with the move and everything."

"I understand. I don't think Laura's going to go off and live with Ben any time soon, but I'd like them to keep in touch. She needs some contact, and to be honest, so does he. They might need each other in the future. I'd like to get things settled before I go."

"Oh, I don't know how I'll manage without you now. You've been such a friend, so you have."

"You'll be fine. You won't lose Laura, you'll gain Isobel."

"I'd like to get to know Isobel and it's going well. Actually, much better than I hoped, but, but..." She stopped again, overcome by tears. "I don't know what's got into me," Fid said apologetically.

"Perhaps you should see the doctor. You might be anaemic or something. You look pale."

"Come to think of it, I don't feel too good."

Angela stared into Fid's eyes. "When's your period due?"

"Oh, I don't have periods, Angela. I had one or two after that morning-after pill you gave me when I slept with Ron, but then nothing. That's normal for me. They're few and far between."

"I think you should do a test."

"Ok, I'll go to the doctor's. Not having a period every month isn't unusual to me. I suppose he'll test me for anaemia."

"I meant a test for pregnancy. I've got a test in the drawer. It's an essential piece of equipment when dealing with teenagers."

Five minutes later, Fid's world turned upside down. She stared speechlessly at the blue line.

Angela smiled maternally. "I've had four kids, so I recognise the symptoms. I'm exactly the same for the first three months."

Somehow, Fid found her voice. "I never thought this would happen to me."

172

"Sometimes, the hormones in the pill you took can trigger a normal cycle after the induced one. If there was something wrong before, perhaps it has cured it. Every cloud, eh?"

"Please don't say anything to anyone else yet. I had a miscarriage last time. That was fifteen years ago."

"It's alright. I'm not allowed to gossip about my charges. Or their foster parents, for that matter."

"Thanks for that. And thanks for everything. You've been great, so you have." Fid felt near to tears a second time. This was so hard to take in. "What would I do without you, Angela?"

"You're going to have to do without me, I'm afraid. I'd like to make some provision for Laura until she's eighteen, but as soon as that's in place, I'll go. I'm needed to look after grandchildren. I've lots of plans."

"I'll miss you so much."

"I know you'll be alright. You've so many good things to look forward to. Now take the day off and go to the doctor's. You can catch up tomorrow."

Head reeling, stomach churning, knees trembling, Fid did as she was told.

# CHAPTER 40

## *May 1993*

Life for Isobel wasn't so bad after all. There was a permanent uneasy feeling in the back of her mind, and it came to the fore whenever her parentage or that of other people was mentioned. She was a stranger to herself and it felt very lonely. But everyday routine went on as usual. Dad, Teddy and school were the same as ever.

Laura and her friends became Isobel's friends and even Fid and Sean stopped staring at her inanely every time they bumped into her at the cottage. The den became her hideout and, although at times it felt weird, she was living with the insecurity of who she really was. Occasionally, she realised that Laura must be experiencing the same problems, but it never occurred to her to share thoughts about it. Laura always seemed so confident.

When Dad told her he was off to London to exhibit his paintings, she was quite pleased to have the flat to herself for once. Unfortunately, he'd already given Molly, their neighbour in the downstairs flat, some money as a contribution to food, and Molly had agreed to take Isobel in.

There was a list of instructions written by Dad about the doors being kept locked after she went into the flat for any reason, switching lights out, turning taps off, bin collection and other boring things. She put the list in the pocket of her jeans, then forgot which jeans she was wearing at the time. But she was sure Molly would remind her, anyway.

The day before he was due to leave, there was a knock on the door. Dad was out taking an evening class.

"Hi, is Ben in?" It was Molly with an envelope in her hand.

"He's at work. He'll be back around ten."

"Tell him I'm sorry it's such short notice, but I can't have you to stay. Sam's got a contract in Cornwall and they want him straightaway. We're going tomorrow morning at five o'clock."

Isobel tried to sound disappointed. "Don't worry, it'll be ok. I'll stay at Teddy's."

Molly handed over the envelope, which contained fifty pounds.

"Oh thanks," Isobel said as nonchalantly as she could manage. This was great news.

She was eager to get her dad out of the house the following morning, which was Saturday.

Luckily, he didn't notice that next door's car was missing. She waved him off in the old Ford Escort estate which had replaced the Hillman Imp when it fell to bits. The back seats were down, and the space was stuffed with paintings of every size and shape.

Her next move was to race round to Laura's as soon as the car was out of sight. All the friends had planned to meet at the den in order to discuss holiday jobs at Woolworth's and Tesco's. But as Isobel now had the house to herself and some money, more exciting activities sprang to mind.

"We can have a party. I've got enough to buy pizzas and hot dogs and cola. There's six bottles of wine that's been in the cupboard for ages."

"Won't your Dad notice they're gone?" asked Teddy.

"I'll buy some more when I get a summer job. He never looks in that cupboard. I'll go to the town square and McDonald's to invite people. Loads of my classmates are in there on Saturday mornings."

"Yea, mine too," added Laura. "There might be some cans of cider still in the boxes of kitchen stuff we've not unpacked yet."

"What about music? Can you bring your ghetto blaster and some cassettes?" asked Isobel.

"I'll bring all the tapes I've got," Laura assured her.

After the visit to the town square and McDonald's,

Isobel headed home, spending most of the fifty pounds on route.

She pushed the furniture in the living room against the walls to make a dance floor and spread out food and drink in the kitchen. Laura turned up early with the promised tapes, portable music player and cider. She was wearing a pair of silky shorts and some shiny red boots. Her black wavy hair hung around her face. Isobel felt envious. Laura looked gorgeous.

All that was left to do was await the guests. And they came. Soon the place was alive with music. Everyone was singing and dancing along to Wham and Duran Duran. Donald and Nighat seemed to have taken a shine to each other. Isobel saw them dancing and laughing together and wondered why she'd never noticed it before. Their relationship was so unlike hers and Teddy's. Teddy never gazed into her eyes like Donald was gazing at Nighat. There was nothing in the least romantic about her friendship with Teddy. They were too used to each other. Suddenly, she felt envious. Perhaps a real boyfriend might come along for her sometime.

However, the party was a big success. Everyone was enjoying themselves. Someone put on 'Achy Breaky Heart' and the whole room joined in with the words at the top of their voices. People helped themselves to food and drink and forgot about school and their exams. Above the din, Sarah yelled into Isobel's ear, "What's Woody doing here?"

"Who?"

"You remember, the guy who threw milk shake all over you in Mc Donald's. I've just seen him. I'm sure it was Woody. I'd recognise him anywhere."

Isobel looked round, but there was no sign of him anywhere. "You're certain?"

Sarah nodded vigorously.

At that moment, Isobel heard a singer hit a high note, then another, out of time and out of tune. "Someone's screaming!" said Isobel. She looked around. Her bedroom door was shut. It was never closed; the catch was broken because she'd slammed it so many times. Without thinking, she ran over and pushed the door with all her strength. It didn't budge, but she could hear the screams more clearly. Panic gripped her and she banged on it with both hands. Then Teddy was at her side, pushing with his back and shoulders. There was something heavy against the door.

With a great effort they opened the door a few inches. It was enough to see Woody standing over Laura, who was pinned to the side of the bed by her shoulders, and her arms and legs were flailing in every direction. Somehow they forced their way in. There was a chest of drawers in the way. Woody turned as the door opened and in that distracted moment, Laura landed a kick behind his knee. His legs buckled and Isobel and Teddy grabbed him.

He jabbed them both with his elbows, but they managed to hold on. Sarah was behind them and, between the three of them, they found the strength to drag him across the living room to the front door. The music was still blaring away as the friends pitched him out.

The party guests stared in horror as Laura staggered after them, holding up her silk shorts, now in tatters.

Woody began swearing in a slurred tone, accompanied by thumps on the other side of the door. Isobel started shaking uncontrollably. She leant against the door in order to stay upright. Every blow shook the door and reverberated through her body. She could see Teddy trying to look at Woody through the skylight. Sweat was pouring down his face and arms. Laura was screaming "Piss off! Piss off!" over and over again. Sarah was sitting on the floor, knees under her chin and head in hands.

Then the banging stopped. Nobody dared open the door. Someone turned the music off. Teddy rushed to the front window.

"We'd better call the police," said Donald.

"Please don't. I couldn't stand to talk to them,"

pleaded Laura. "And don't tell your Dad, Izzie. I don't want him to know."

"He'd be proud of you," said Teddy. "You kicked him on his leg and he went off balance, otherwise we'd have never got him off."

"Thank heavens for Doc Martens," answered Laura, looking down at her new boots. "Sean bought me these with his first big wage. But I'm a rubbish shot. I was aiming for his balls."

The friends all laughed, and Laura joined in, but suddenly, Laura's face crumpled and she burst into tears. Sarah put an arm around her and they clung to each other. Teddy shouted from the window. "He's got into a taxi. I've just seen it heading out of town, towards Ashwood. We'd better go, before he comes back. He might have gone to fetch his mates."

"I've nowhere to go. And Laura was supposed to be sleeping here. My Dad will kill me if he finds out about the party." Isobel could only think about the trouble she'd be in.

Laura stopped crying. "Come home with me. We can sleep in the den. I don't want to be on my own. I can't tell Fid and Sean. I don't want them to know."

"Oh, Laura, I'd be so grateful. It's all my fault for having the party in the first place. He didn't touch you down there, did he?"

"No, but he's ripped my new shorts trying."

"Oh, my God!" Isobel froze as the full horror of the situation dawned on her. How could such a happy occasion go so wrong?

The party was over. The guests hurriedly gathered their belongings and set off for the all-night bus into town. Teddy rang for a taxi for himself, Isobel and Laura. The remainder of the fifty pounds would just about cover the cost.

"He can't come for another half hour. Let's get cleaned up, otherwise Ben will know all about it." Teddy, ever the practical one, began collecting rubbish in a black bag.

Isobel tried to make Laura a hot sweet tea for shock, but there was no milk left and someone had spilt the sugar. The pizzas and hot dogs were reduced to a few crumbs on a paper plate on the floor. Somebody had been sick and missed the toilet and the living room smelled of red wine.

Frantically, they restored order before the taxi came. Laura borrowed a skirt, but it was much too big, and they all laughed when she put it on. But Laura's laughter quickly turned to tears again, despite Isobel's and Teddy's efforts to comfort her.

"You were so brave, Laura," Isobel reassured her. "I couldn't have had the bottle to do what you did."

"You were brave too, Izzie," said Teddy. "You ran to that bedroom door without a thought about what was behind it!"

"I didn't have time to think," Isobel replied. She tried to sound nonchalant, but she was thrilled with the praise. Teddy did care about her after all.

The taxi dropped the girls off. There were only three items of furniture in the den: two sofas and an old chest of drawers. Between them, they pushed the chest of drawers against the door and waited for morning. The May dawn came quickly. Isobel gazed out of the tiny window at the sky, counting the colours. Grey, pink, turquoise, blue, white. How could it look so beautiful when she felt so wretched?

She fell asleep for a couple of hours. When she awoke, she could see Sean through the window in the distance, pushing a wheelbarrow across the lawn of the big house. She looked over to Laura. She was curled up on the other sofa with her face to the wall.

"Laura," Isobel whispered in case she was asleep. But she was awake, and turned around, eyes full of tears.

"I was so frightened, Izzie. Don't tell your father. I couldn't bear it."

"I won't. He'll blame me. It's all my fault. He thinks

I'm at Molly's, our neighbour. Have you got any bruises, Laura?"

"I haven't looked." She lifted her sleeves to reveal some ugly red finger marks on her upper arms. "I'll have to keep these out of sight. I can't tell Fid."

"I don't want to go back home, but it's school on Monday. What am I going to do? Dad's not back until tomorrow week."

"Stay with me. I don't want to sleep on my own. I'll ask Sean to get your uniform." Laura had never shown Isobel that she was afraid of anything.

"Thanks, I'd like that. Will Fid and Sean mind?"

"Mind? They're dying to get you in their sights. They're fascinated with you."

"Dad's the same about you. He's so eager to please you, it's embarrassing at times."

"Does it feel strange, not knowing who you really are?" asked Laura.

"Yes, it does," answered Isobel, glad to be able to discuss it with someone. "All my past, my lovely grandparents, pictures of my mum and all the stories about her were all wrong. They're your stories. Dad should tell them to you. He probably hasn't said because he knows I'd be so jealous."

"It was like that for Fid and Sean. They love talking about their best friend. I just couldn't take in that she was a total stranger, and my mother was someone they never met."

"I hated you at first," Isobel confessed. "I knew Dad was so fascinated with you and it hurt so much."

"I was the same," said Laura. "I was sure Sean and Fid would want you much more than I was wanted. But now it's great to have somebody who knows what it's like to be me."

"I feel the same. I've got you to talk to. I was always different to everyone else. They all had mothers and I had just a picture on the wall. Then even that turned out to be someone else's mum."

"I felt like that, too. But I thought I was part of Fid and Sean's life when they were young and actually they are nothing to do with me. It was so hard."

Isobel put a comforting arm around Laura's shoulders. "We won't fall out anymore," she promised.

"Well, we might," said Laura, "but it won't be about this. You're my friend now."

They chatted on for a couple of hours. Isobel found herself revealing all her insecurities about leaving school, about making new friends and having to talk to people she didn't know. Laura seemed to understand, even though she was so confident.

"I was never afraid of anything until that time when Woody got me in your bedroom. Now I know what you mean," Laura's voice was full of understanding. "I always acted first and thought about it later. "My method is to fight back straight away."

"I can't do that. I don't know how to fight back. I wish I did. I can't do horrid things to people because I know how it hurts."

"Well, I'll look out for you from now on, just like you did for me with Woody," replied Laura. "We'd better tell Fid that you're staying over until Ben gets back. I'm sure it will be alright."

Of course, Fid and Sean were delighted to have Isobel stay the week. She didn't mention the party, but just told them that she didn't want to be on her own. That much was true.

She found that there were advantages to living in a house with other women. Fid and Laura were well used to shopping together at Sunday markets, wandering around looking for bargains, something that neither Teddy nor Ben were willing to do. It was great to walk around without being nagged to hurry up. Fid taught her lots of new dishes to cook and was sympathetic when Isobel's period started. Both Fid and Sean told her stories about her mother's teenage years and the things they did together during Laurel's short life. She was fascinated, but it was hard to comprehend that it was anything to do with her. At least it distracted her from the horrible events at the party.

Daytimes were bearable, even enjoyable. But at bedtime it all came flooding back. Sean had put a camp bed next to Laura's and they whispered together in their room, going over and over the drama. Strange dreams haunted her nights and she dreaded going home. Laura seemed so brave, and Isobel could only imagine what she was going through.

All too soon, the week came to an end. There was a knock on the door on Sunday evening. It was Ben. He explained that he rang Teddy when he found Molly's flat empty, and Teddy told him where Isobel was. He was friendly and polite to the Flanagans, but Isobel could tell immediately that there was something up. He didn't speak at all on the drive home.

When they entered the flat, he stood silently in the middle of the living room. Eventually, he said "I'm waiting."

"What for?"

"An explanation for this, for a start."

Too late, Isobel noticed a red wine stain on the carpet that she'd overlooked.

"I assume it was this." He opened the cupboard which once contained six bottles of burgundy. "And here's some more of it." He opened the bathroom door to reveal trickles of a red substance congealed on the pedestal of the toilet. "You can't be trusted for one week!"

'Oh God, we made a bad job of cleaning up,' thought Isobel. "Sorry, Dad," she muttered, head down.

"Sorry? You will be, lady. And what's happened to the front door?"

He opened the door to show chipped paintwork and splinters. "And I wonder what's in the bin?" He ran down the stairs and disappeared into the yard below. "Now we'll see what you've been up to," he shouted as he came back with a black bin bag.

'If only I'd remembered what day to put the bins out,' thought Isobel.

Ben began rummaging through the rubbish. "Yes, I thought so," he said triumphantly as he pulled out several empty cider cans. "What made you think that..." His voice tailed off as he found a pair of tattered satin shorts tangled up with a pizza box. He picked up the ragged remains with his fingertips, turning them over to see where they were ripped.

He stared at Isobel, shock and anguish on his face.

"They're not mine, Dad," she heard herself say. "They're Laura's.

# CHAPTER 41

Laura was in the kitchen with Fid, preparing the evening meal. Sean's parents were coming round to eat with them. Isobel had left only a couple of hours ago, but she was missing her already.

It was hard to keep recent events to herself. She chatted on about nothing while Fid kneaded pastry and peeled vegetables. Luckily, Fid seemed preoccupied and didn't notice. The knock on the door was no surprise, although Brendan and Bridie usually came in by the back door, which was always unlocked during the day.

Laura turned round from her task to see Ben and Isobel standing in the kitchen doorway. "Come in," she heard Sean say as he ushered them into the room. "If it's tea you're wanting, you're just in time, so you are." But Laura looked into Ben's eyes and knew immediately why they were there.

"I didn't say anything, Laura, honest! He found the shorts. He'd guessed about the party and looked in the bin." Fid and Sean were staring at her now. Suddenly she felt a cold shiver run through her body. "He only wants to help." Isobel's voice was pleading for forgiveness.

"I thought Fid and Sean should know." Ben's tone was calm at that point. "I didn't want to break confidences, but this is too big for you girls to handle on your own."

All the tensions of the past week suddenly welled up inside Laura, and for the second time since the attack, she started sobbing uncontrollably. She looked up to see Fid and Sean's stricken faces, but she couldn't stop.

She heard Isobel tell the story, but it was as if she was talking about a stranger. The back door opened, and Laura raced out of the kitchen and out through the front door before she had to face Brendan and Bridie. Safe in the den, she lay on the settee, reliving the horror. After a while, the door opened and Isobel came in, carrying a tray with a bowl of stew and a piece of pie.

"I told him not to come round, but he wouldn't listen. I'm so sorry. He wants to go and look for Woody and drag him to the police station by his hair. Sean just wants to punch him. They're both shouting at Fid because she doesn't want them to do anything. Dad usually goes quiet when he's angry. I've never seen him like this."

Laura stopped crying. "It's not your fault. But I don't want to talk to them about it."

"Do you want to tell me anything?" Isobel asked.

"Not really. You know everything anyway. I'd like you to stay for a bit, though. We could play some music."

Isobel put a cassette in the machine and they sat together listening to George Michael. Eventually, Ben appeared at the den to take Isobel home. His face looked tired and drawn.

"You've been a very brave girl, just like my Karen. She'd have been so proud of you."

Laura somehow managed a smile. "Thanks," was all she could think of to say.

She waited until she heard Brendan and Bridie leave before she wandered back into the kitchen. Fid held out her arms, and despite herself, Laura ran into them.

"We know all about that carry on in McDonald's, so we do." Sean's voice had a strange quiver which Laura had never heard before. "You were wonderful to stand up for Isobel. But you put yourself in so much danger. We'll have to go to the police. We can't let him get away with it."

"Please, please don't! I can't tell anyone!"

Fid took Laura's side. "The police will go into every detail, Sean. I've read about these things. It's another ordeal for the child."

The three of them discussed the matter of police involvement all evening. After a while, Laura stopped joining in and left Fid and Sean to argue. This was bad enough in her own home. What would it be like in the police station?

At last, it was bedtime. Fid and Sean both hugged her goodnight just like they did when she was small. She was about to climb the stairs when Fid said, "Bridie brought a letter round. It's been in the shed for months, apparently. Brendan took it in there and then forgot all about it. It's addressed to me." She took a grubby envelope from her pocket. "What the bejasus is this? Where's this come from?"

It was a cheque for two thousand pounds. The covering letter said it was a prize for the hairdressing competition Fid had entered in Birmingham. There was also an invitation to work at the show next November.

"What a lovely surprise!" Laura was grateful to be able to lift the mood.

"It's nice to have a bit of good news," said Fid. "I've got better news to tell you, but I was saving it until I was sure it wasn't going to end in disappointment."

"What could be better than the money and the job into the bargain?" Sean looked puzzled.

"I'm pregnant, Sean. I'm three months gone. And past the danger time."

Laura watched Sean's face light up.

"I can't believe it! It's a miracle, so it is!"

"I didn't want to tell you until it was well on its way, just in case. But it's cheering up we all need, to be sure. With a bit of luck, we'll have a baby for Christmas."

"It's great news!" said Laura.

"To be sure, it is," Fid replied. "But it's been a bitter-sweet day for us. It certainly isn't the way I wanted to tell you."

But Laura was thrilled and, for a change, went to bed with something nice to think about.

# CHAPTER 42

It was the last day of the summer half-term. Laura, Nighat and Sarah were all going to the same sixth-form college, but the rest of their classmates were to be scattered all over the town. They would meet up for exams, but otherwise five years of being classmates had come to an end. By coincidence, Teddy, Isobel and the twins were going to the same college as Laura. For the first time since they'd met, they would all be attending the same school.

The friends had planned to meet up at Laura's after their leaving day. Ben was insisting that Isobel paid back the stolen fifty pounds she had used for the party, so Sean offered to pay her for some work on the mansion garden.

Laura hung around the shopping precinct in case Isobel appeared, so they could walk together. She was aware that Isobel often went that way. Eventually, she came, and they set off to Laura's along the pedestrianised street, looking in shop windows and gossiping.

As they approached a cash machine, Laura noticed a young man, about twenty years old, trying to use his card. He was struggling to put in the right numbers. At last, he succeeded and stood back from the machine, staring at the screen. Impulsive as ever, she was about to offer help when a man walked up, knocked him to the ground and pressed the keys. The girls watched as the man extracted a handful of notes.

"Hey, you! Get off him!" she yelled as the boy tried to get up. The man kicked the boy before turning round towards Laura and Isobel. Laura's heart froze as she once more stared into Woody's face. Before Laura could think what to do, he lunged at her.

"Laura, run!" Isobel grabbed her arm and they raced down the precinct, dodging shoppers as they went. Isobel's long legs were much faster than Laura's, so she was almost dragged along. She heard footsteps running behind her. Fear gave her strength to run faster, but they were getting louder. Panic gripped them both. Isobel's hand gripped her tighter and they stumbled on, gasping with the exertion.

Then someone shouted "Laura! Izzie!" There was something familiar about the voice. It took a nanosecond to realise it was Teddy's.

"Stop! Wait! It's alright. Look!" he pointed behind them. In the distance, she saw Woody, small as a toy soldier, struggling between two burly men.

"He was racing after you, but those men caught him. You're safe."

It took a second or two to process this, then Laura felt an enormous wave of relief. Suddenly, she realised that she was totally exhausted. Her legs turned to jelly, and Teddy and Isobel propped her up on either side. Memories of Woody's face came into her mind. She could see him staring down at her. She began to feel nauseous, recalling the smell of his sweat, his greasy clothes, the beer on his warm breath. She could feel her own racing heartbeats and she was gasping for breath. Somehow, they arrived at the cottage to be greeted by a horrified Fid.

"Jesus, Mary and Joseph! What in heaven's name have you done this time?" She ushered a dishevelled Laura into the house and sat her down at the kitchen table.

"She saw someone being robbed and she tried to stop it, but the thief turned out to be Woody," Isobel told her.

"Yes, then Izzie dragged her away, otherwise she might have got hurt," added Teddy. "He chased them, but luckily, someone caught him."

"For God's sake, when are you going to learn to leave things alone? Don't tell Sean, he'll be out there trying to strangle him. He'd have never hurt a fly until Woody came on the scene."

"It's ok, they've got him, I'm sure," Teddy reassured her.

Fid applied first aid in the form of mugs of tea and plates of hot potato cakes. Soon, Laura's young body replenished its energy levels. By the time the rest of the gang turned up the trio were sufficiently rested to start work in the garden of the mansion. Sean set them a task and soon they were clearing a vast field of weeds which had once been a lawn in front of the big house. They sat outside to devour sandwiches and homemade cakes and, slowly, Laura began to calm down. She saw Sean hand over the fifty pounds to Isobel. Isobel hugged him in delight and Laura felt a pang of jealousy. But she watched Sean's face light up and couldn't help feeling pleased for him.

"Can I tell Dad about this?" Isobel asked before she left.

"I suppose he'll get to know eventually, but don't tell him yet. I bet he'll be straight round here. There was such a fuss last time I don't think I could cope at the moment."

The next morning Laura woke up feeling anxious with no idea why. Then it dawned on her. The elation she'd felt at breaking up from school had disintegrated like tissue paper in the rain. She'd never known fear before, but she was frightened of Woody. She stayed in bed until she heard Sean set off to work in the gardens.

Over breakfast, she confided in Fid. "I don't want to go out anywhere in case I bump into that lunatic. I had lots of plans. There's the cinema, the park, the shops. He could pop up anywhere. What am I going to do? I should be meeting the gang this afternoon. I daren't go."

"Sure, you've had a terrible shock, but you'll get over it. Teddy said those men caught him."

"Yes, but we don't know what happened next. Where is he now?"

"I could get Sean to go with you anywhere you wanted to go."

"I'm not walking around with Sean in tow.    How would that look? I'd rather stop in."

Fid had a more practical solution. "Perhaps your friends can come here. You're safe in the den, so you are. Why not ring them?"

It seemed better than moping in the house. Sarah and the twins brought crisps, Nighat contributed her mum's homemade samosas, and Teddy and Isobel provided the latest music. The day passed pleasantly enough. Sean saw them hanging about and took advantage to offer them more work on the gardens. They all promised to return the next day.

"It's lucky you are to have such good friends, Laura. They're happy to spend their time out here, if you ask me."

"They're after the money," she replied, but she was comforted by the fact that they were willing to dig and weed instead of going into town to do more exciting things.

The next day, Teddy arrived with a newspaper cutting. He read it aloud to the friends and Fid, who were gathered in the den.

"*A CARELESS CARER CAUSES CHAOS*. That's the headline. *A social worker who was training a young man in life skills took his eye off his charge while chatting to a friend. The boy, who suffers from Down's syndrome, was in the town centre to learn how to use a cash machine. His carer, who is said to be devastated, was only a few feet away when his charge was mugged by a thief who stole two hundred pounds from the boy's account as soon as he logged in his code. The thug then knocked the boy down, kicked him and made off with the money. The carer and his friend pursued the thief and managed to detain him until the police arrived. The victim is in hospital and his condition is said to be stable. The alleged assailant already has a suspended sentence and is now in custody, awaiting a trial.*

"See, he's banged up now. You're safe."

"I can't go out, Teddy. I'll be watching for him all the time," answered Laura.

"He's in jail, Laura," said Nighat. "He's going nowhere."

But Laura was not convinced. "They might let him out. You never know."

"It won't be long till you're back to normal," Fid reassured her. "It's peace and quiet you're wanting now."

Laura wanted to believe this, but part of her knew she'd never be the same bold, happy-go-lucky girl she was before the fateful party.

"That's odd." Fid picked up a letter from the table. "This is from Angela, inviting me to a meeting at the children's home. I'll be there anyway. Why send for me?"

"Oh, perhaps it's about the adoption," said Laura.

"What do you know about that? Holy Mary, didn't I ask Angela not to say anything without telling me first?"

"She didn't say anything, Fid. Izzie told me."

Fid turned to Isobel. "And how did you find out?"

"I read the letter to Dad. It was lying around on the desk at home."

"It's ok, I don't mind. I can still live here, and I've got a grant till I'm eighteen. Then I can do what I want."

"You can stay at ours sometimes, and I can stay here if I'm allowed," added Isobel.

Fid stared from one girl to the other, completely lost for words.

# CHAPTER 43

It was Angela's last day as a social worker. Fid went to work as usual, but her heart was heavy. There was no way she could burden her with Laura's experiences, although the child was legally Angela's responsibility and by rights should be told. Instead, she chatted amiably about the progress of the big house and the cottage.

"And we've got a bit more money. I won a prize for the best hairdo at the beauty fair last November. The cheque's been in Brendan's shed since before we left. I banked it straightaway in case I forgot and let it expire. There's an invite to the next show, but I won't be going, to be sure."

"That's really good, Fid. Congratulations."

"It's a bit suspicious I am, to be honest. I'm not convinced it's genuine."

"You're a good hairdresser, everyone says so. It might not be anything to do with that man you slept with. It could be from the absent father, as hush money."

"Carl swore he'd never admit to it. Threats are more his style, not bribes. Sean was there when I opened the envelope. I daren't raise any doubts in his mind."

"I'm glad you didn't tell Sean about the affair. He doesn't deserve to suffer. Anyway, it could be simply that you were the best hairdresser."

"I think he's aware that something changed after I went away. He's not sure what." Fid sighed softly. She hated deceiving Sean, but it was better than hurting him. And maybe she did win the competition fair and square. Who was to know?

"I've got Ben Moss coming in later, which is why you got an official invitation to the office. We need to discuss things together. He's happy with my proposal to adopt Laura, but I've not spoken to her about it yet. I wanted your input first."

"Too late," replied Fid. "The girls have already

approved it and worked out the details themselves. Apparently, Isobel read your letter and told Laura what was in it. They've decided to spend some time at mine together, some time at Ben's together and some time apart."

"We seem to be superfluous, Fid." Angela was philosophical. "I've started the proceedings now, and it will go forward without me. My work is done."

"Thank you so much, Angela. You've been wonderful and I can't thank you enough. When Laura first came to me my biggest fear was that she would leave us to be adopted by another family who lived miles away and we'd never see her again. Ben's a nice man and we get on well. If she's going anywhere, I'd have chosen him, even if he wasn't her father. I can't imagine how he must be feeling. It's desperate we are to get close to Isobel, so it must be a thousand times worse for him. He's every right to his daughter, but he has to seek permission."

"Even so, he's got the chance of a relationship with her. It's turned out much better than I hoped," said Angela, beaming across at Fid.

Fid began to feel less guilty about concealing the troubles with Woody. After all, it was Angela's last day. Why spoil it?

When Ben arrived he was totally in agreement with the girls' plans.

"There's one thing we never foresaw in this whole situation," he told Angela. "Laura and Izzie are very close friends. They seem to have an empathy with each other that we adults had no part in. I'm not sure how it developed but it's helped them to deal with their problems. We're so lucky that they found their own solutions."

Angela smiled. "They're so lucky that you two let them."

"We didn't have a choice," said Fid. "To be sure, I hadn't a clue what to do with Laura. She coped with it all in her own way."

"I'd have to say the same. And it's a strange situation for me. I'll be adopting my natural child, and my legal daughter is someone else's."

"I know they'll be staying at each other's houses, so we'll both see them a lot," Fid reassured him.

"I have a request to make. I thought it best to ask first before I told Izzie about it."

"Well, ask away. That's what this meeting's for," said Angela. "In fact, it's your last chance. This is my last working day, and I intend to stick to that."

"Good on you, Angela. Has Laura got a passport?"

"Yes, I got her one so she could go on school trips. It's quite a chore to obtain for children in care, and I didn't want her to miss out. But she never used it."

"Isobel's got one because we planned to go to Jamaica with my parents. But my father was always too frail to make the journey."

"Why do you need to know?" said Fid.

"I have a chance to go to New York for three months. I have a friend who's offered a gallery to me for the summer. I'm taking Isobel and I'd like your permission to take Laura as well. I'll look after her, and there are some jobs they can do to keep them out of trouble. They'll be with me all the time." His eyes pleaded his case. "They will have to be back before me as my college starts two weeks later than theirs. I'm hoping that Izzie can live at yours for that time." He looked imploringly at both women.

Fid was silent for a moment. Three months seemed such a long time. But if it would take Laura away from the experiences with Woody which had sapped her confidence, perhaps it would help. At least she wouldn't be looking over her shoulder. And it would be nice to have Isobel in the house again.

"I think I can give permission," Angela answered. "But I'll respect whatever Fid wants. After all, she's the one who brought Laura up."

Although Fid's heart was turning over at the idea of her lovely Laura on the other side of the world, she knew she had to say yes. Maybe Laura would come back as her old, confident self again. Soon, she'd be eighteen and making her own decisions.

"If she wants to go, I won't try to stop her."

Ben hugged Fid with tears in his eyes. "Izzie really enjoyed her stay with you," he told her. "I didn't know how much she needed female company. I've never been able to provide a mother figure for her."

"She has one now, so she has, if she wants one. I promised her mother I'd help look after her. If I can play a small part in her life..."

Just then a member of staff knocked on the door. "We've made some tea. Would you come to the dining room?"

They all followed the carer to find the children lined up in their best clothes waiting to give Angela homemade cards and presents. The youngest child came forward with a huge bunch of sweet-scented flowers. Angela looked overcome with gratitude and sadness and mumbled, "Thank you. I'll miss you all so much."

Fid went home thinking about Angela and the first time they met. The job certainly wouldn't be the same anymore. She knew it was the beginning of many changes. The baby was due in November. Maybe it was time to go. Working at the orphanage had been great since Angela came, but it was time to move on. She still had her mobile hairdressing kit and the products from the salon. She could take the baby with her. This would be a new life for herself and Sean in so many different ways. At least they would have more time to spend together.

# CHAPTER 44

Ben drove home feeling elated and anxious at the same time. He was taking two sixteen-year-old girls to a foreign place with only one friend in the entire country. And that person didn't like children, let alone teenagers. There was no hope of any support from Rona if things got difficult. He had no idea how much time Rona would spend with him when Laura and Isobel were in tow. But it was exciting. He couldn't wait to share the adventure with his daughters. It felt like a family holiday already.

He didn't mind that Rona had no plans for joining his family. It certainly wouldn't be on the cards now this had increased. It had hurt him terribly before, but, strangely, he found he could live with it after the turmoil of the recent months. Sometimes, he found it hard to believe that nine months had passed since that day Fid and Laura walked into his home. Other days, he felt he'd known Laura all her young life. Yet there was so much more he wanted to find out. He'd like to love her as much as he loved Izzie, but he wasn't sure that was possible. He and his little girl had been through everything together. They had sixteen years of shared history. But he'd try his best. He owed it to Karen.

He didn't let on to Fid or Angela, but the contract in New York could be quite lucrative. Rona was pleased with his support in London and the week had gone well. Although there was no romance when he was down there, they became closer and more trusting of each other. Nevertheless, he was surprised when she called him to offer him three months in a gallery close to hers. He had to accept. At best, the relationship might develop again. At worst, he'd make some money. And, if Isobel didn't find out how much, he might manage to keep hold of it. Suddenly, he realised there'd be two teenagers now trying to spend his money for him. Perhaps the extra cash would be much needed.

He'd planned the trip for a week hence, when the last GCSE was taken. It would all be very last-minute, as he hadn't even mentioned it to the girls yet. Visas, clothes, suitcases would all have to be sourced within a few days. It occurred to Ben that Laura might have plans that couldn't be cancelled. He couldn't waste time. He'd have to ask her tomorrow. He hoped against hope she would agree. If she refused, there was no plan B. Isobel would probably kick up a fuss, Rona would still expect him there on the dot, and he would have less than a week to work something out. But she'd want to come. Wouldn't she?

The day after the meeting, Laura let herself be dragged to McDonald's with Teddy, Isobel and Sarah. At first, she looked round anxiously every time the door opened, but gradually, the gossip and banter from the others relaxed her enough to enjoy the visit.

"This is where Fid and Sean used to come with Izzie's real Mum and Dad," Laura informed them all.

"How do you know that?" Teddy asked with interest.

"Fid told me all about it. I've got lots of stories. I'll have to pass them on to you, Izzie. They're all about their fabulous Saturdays, the only day they were both free. They hadn't got half the things we've got. The cinema was exciting for them."

"Fid filled me in on quite a few tales of their youth. It's fascinating, but it's really strange too," replied Isobel.

"Imagine how I felt when I first saw that picture on your wall?"

"I can't," answered Isobel. "I wish I could. But I know when you brought that photo of my parents round to our flat, it blew my mind."

Laura shot a look of sympathy across to Isobel but there was no need for words. Soon, the conversation became more general and turned to films, music and summer holidays. Sean was still working on the gardens at the mansion and the friends decided to return to the den to ask for some work. Nighat and the twins had promised to join them there later in the day. The twins appeared soon after the others got there.

"Laura, I've got something for you." Don handed her a letter, avoiding her eyes. He seemed much very subdued, which was unlike him. He was usually lively and cheerful.

Laura opened the note.

*Sorry but I won't be able to see you again. Dad caught me and Don snogging in the garage when he walked me home on Saturday. He's forbidden me to see him and won't let me out of the house. He's locked the garage door so I can't sneak away anymore. I'm going to Scotland to be married to my cousin next month.*

*Love to Izzie, Teddy and Sarah.*

*Nighat xx*

Speechless, Laura handed the note to Izzie. She couldn't imagine life without Nighat. They'd been friends ever since they met on their first day at big school. Until she got the den, all homework, leisure activities and gossiping had taken place in Nighat's bedroom. How had this happened? But she remembered Don and Nighat laughing at each other's jokes and dancing with each other. Laura wondered why she'd never noticed they were a couple. The gang did everything together, or so she thought.

Don was curled up on the settee, being comforted by Isobel.

"I didn't know you two were so close," Laura said, apologetically. "I thought I knew Nighat so well."

"I noticed," said Isobel. "It was such a different thing to me and Teddy, that's why."

"Well, that's because we're so used to each other," protested Teddy. "We don't need to be doing that romantic stuff. I can't do with that rubbish. It's stupid."

"Oh, shut up, Teddy!" Isobel replied. "Can't you see how upset he is? We're not all like you."

Don got up to leave.

"I'll come home with you," offered Phil.

"No, it's ok. I'd rather be on my own for a bit."

"I can't imagine sitting in here without Nighat." Sarah

said, sadly "Fancy not being allowed to say goodbye."

"I can't believe it either. I want to go to Scotland to search for her. I know she's got some cousins up in Glasgow. I bet they've taken her off already. I can't believe she's being married off to one of them." Don's voice was almost a whisper.

"We'll miss her too, Don. In fact, it doesn't seem real. I think she'll walk in and tell us it's all a joke." Isobel put an arm round Don as she spoke, but he remained stiff and unresponsive to the comfort.

"There'll be plenty of girls at college," said Sarah.

"I don't want anyone else. I only want her."

"Are you sure you don't want me to come home with you?" Phil asked again.

"Let him go, Phil," Teddy interrupted.

Don wandered off. The rest watched his dejected back view disappear down the road. No one spoke for a minute or two, then Sarah remembered the plans for working on the garden.

"I'll go and get Sean," said Laura, running into the house. She was glad of something to do. The news about Nighat threw up so many unanswered questions that she'd rather cope with some other time. All she could think about at the moment was the empty space in her life where her lovely friend had been. It was the last thing she'd expected. In her most bizarre dreams she would never have seen this coming. Her thoughts turned to that first day at school, when she and Nighat compared pencil cases and swapped their stories. It really hurt that they hadn't been allowed to say goodbye to each other.

Sean was sitting in the den with the teenagers, discussing possible weeding and hoeing work when Ben turned up. "I thought you might be in here." He was smiling as if he had a secret.

"What do you want?" said Isobel ungraciously.

"It's alright, I'm not staying long. I've got a request to make. I'm going to New York for the summer to look after a gallery for three months. It's very short notice, but

199

would you like to come with us?" He looked across at Laura nervously.

"Us? Who says I'm going?" Isobel said indignantly.

"There's no way I'm leaving you behind after the last fiasco. You can't be trusted."

"That was just one mistake! Anyway, why didn't you ask me first?"

"I'm not giving you the chance to turn it down. It's..."

"Yes! The answer's 'yes', I'll come!" Laura interrupted the argument. After the shocking news about Nighat, a change might be needed. To get away for a while would be a great adventure. Her impulsive nature was thrilled at the idea. "I'll be back in time for Fid's baby, won't I?"

"Yes, I believe so. I may have to go back occasionally over the winter, but Fid and Sean are happy for Izzie to stay here."

"We'll be glad to have her, to be sure," said Sean.

"I hope they don't fall out after spending so much time together. They need to be back two weeks before me to start sixth-form college and I'm hoping they can stay for that time, as well."

"If there's any shenanigans we've got a spare room. But I'll keep an eye on them. There's plenty of work to do so they won't have time to get up to mischief."

"Hmm, if Laura's coming, I suppose it will be alright." Isobel was grudgingly interested.

"You lucky cows!" said Teddy enviously. "I've never been farther than Italy. I'll be going back there in August, but only for a week."

"God, we've never been farther than Manchester! Don will probably try to wangle a trip to Scotland in case we bump into Nighat, but that's as exciting as it gets!" Phil beamed admiringly at the two adventurers.

"I'm off to a holiday camp somewhere in a forest," Sarah joined in. "Dad fancies it because you ride around on bikes and do sports. It sounds ghastly! I think it's called Center Parcs."

"There's one other thing," Ben interrupted. "Before

she left, your social worker applied for me to adopt you, Laura. It won't make much difference, you can still live here until you're eighteen, but I'll be your guardian if you need me."

It was far from her dreams of being whisked away to a luxury home by a glamorous executive father, but Ben was nice and so was Isobel. In fact, Izzie was the only person who understood how she felt now, just as Nighat understood when they both started high school.

"I knew about it anyway, but, yes, that's ok." She didn't notice how pleased and relieved Ben looked.

The trip was planned for the following week when the last exam was over. Visas and suitcases needed to be organised within a few days.

"Don't pack many clothes because I'll need all our luggage allowance for canvases," warned Ben. "You'll have to buy what you need out there."

"What? They get to choose fashionable clothes in New York?" Sarah was consumed with jealousy. "Well, don't worry about us. We'll be weeding in the garden all summer, that's if Sean gives us the job."

The next few days were hectic and neither the girls nor Ben had time to wonder about the big step they were taking. In no time at all, they found themselves at the airport, with a few belongings and their passports.

The gang came to see them off, driven by Sean in the rundown old van. Don hugged them both, clinging until the last minute. Brendan and Bridie innocently brought food for the journey, unaware that it would be taken away. Fid wiped a tear from her eye, which she blamed on her hormones. Even the unromantic Teddy brought a flower to give to Isobel. He didn't tell her he'd found it on the way.

Everyone waved from the barrier until the girls disappeared down the corridor to the customs. "See you in three months!" they called excitedly to one another.

After the customs check, Ben tried to calm things down. He found a table and left the teenagers sitting there with the flight bags. "I'll get some drinks. What would you like?"

"Can I have a coke, Dad?" asked Isobel.

Without thinking, Laura shouted, "I'll have a coke, too, Dad."

Ben's heart swelled with happiness, but he knew not to make too much of it. He might embarrass Laura. He merely said, "Ok, then," and turned to the counter so that she didn't see the delight on his face.

A woman sitting next to them was listening to the conversation. "Are you going to New York?"

"Yes, first time abroad," Isobel answered.

"Oh! That's where I'm going. And how old are you?"

"We're both sixteen. We were born on the same day."

"You don't look like twins."

"Oh, we're not," said Laura. "We're no relation."

At that moment, Ben signalled to them to come to him.

"Ok, Dad!" they called in unison, grabbing their bags and running across to him.

"Bye!" shouted Isobel over her shoulder to their confused companion. "See you in New York!"

With that, they hurried after Ben on their way to their big adventure.

*Once upon a time, there were two girls*
*who met briefly on the day they were born,*
*then never again for almost sixteen years,*
*when their lives became inextricably entwined.*

*This was their story.*

Acknowledgements ----To my friends Alice, Janet, Cliff, Karen and Gerald, for their help, their encouragement and their patience, without whom I would never have finished the story.
A special thank you to Oliver, who has restored my confidence a hundred fold.

# Author

Chetty Mobola Christina Reis. Despite the author's first names being Nigerian she has never been to Africa. Born and brought up in Stockport, Greater Manchester, with her white grandmother and mixed-race mother, she knew no other black families and was the only black child in her school.

She has always used stories and poetry as an escape and wrote her first novel aged fifteen. Although she has continued to write ever since, only recently has she shared her work.

The author began her nurse training on her eighteenth birthday before becoming a nurse, a midwife and then a health visitor. She spent her sabbatical leave in India where she taught midwifery to student nurses in a hospital in a crowded inner-city neighbourhood of Chennai.

After taking semiretirement from her post as a health advisor for asylum seekers and travellers, she joined the Society of Medical Writers where her articles, short stories and poems regularly won prizes, many being published in the society's biannual magazine, *The Writer*. In 2011, she was awarded the Society's Wilfred Hopkins Prize for Creative Writing.

Christina is still involved, on a voluntary basis, with the asylum seekers in her area and, as a result, has many friends from all corners of the world.

Her research into the life and conditions of poverty-stricken families in industrial Manchester in the early nineteenth century, together with stories of her grandmother's harsh childhood, resulted in a play which was commended in a competition.

The author brought up five children as a single parent, so writing became a luxury retreat, for many years, to offset a stressful job and sometimes an equally stressful home life. Now, able to choose her leisure activities, she finds that still enjoys creating the written word just as much.

As well as *No Relation*, she has completed *So This is England* and is currently writing her third novel, *Relative Strangers*.

Christina's poems have been included in several anthologies, and, for the Society of Medical Writers, she co-edited and contributed to *Poets on Prescription*, a collection of poems inspired by the experiences of health care workers.

Lightning Source UK Ltd.
Milton Keynes UK
UKHW011810310821
389796UK00003B/281